IRISH POETRY

FROM THE ENGLISH INVASION TO 1798

Irish Poetry

from the English Invasion

to 1798

BY

RUSSELL K. ALSPACH
United States Military Academy

Philadelphia

UNIVERSITY OF PENNSYLVANIA PRESS

Second Edition, Revised
© 1959 by the Trustees of the University of Pennsylvania
Copyright, 1943, University of Pennsylvania Press
Published in Great Britain, India, and Pakistan
by the Oxford University Press
London, Bombay, and Karachi
Library of Congress Catalog Card Number: 59-13437
Printed in the United States of America

First printing January 1960
Second printing March 1964

To

CATHARINE

Preface

THIS book is a history of Irish poetry from the English invasion of 1167 to the closing years of the eighteenth century. My purpose is twofold: to tell the story, from the English invasion to the abortive rebellion of 1798, of the poetry written in English in Ireland that can with justice be called "Irish"; and to show how the stories of Irish mythology and the material of Gaelic poetry were put into English during the sixteenth, seventeenth, and eighteenth centuries, thereby bringing about an Irish poetry more distinctively Irish than anything that had gone before and ultimately giving to William Butler Yeats and his fellow poets much of their inspiration.

The likelihood of a confusion of meaning is ever-present in a title such as "Irish Poetry." And yet that title seems a logical one in view of the other chief possibilities: "Irish Poetry in English" and "Anglo-Irish Poetry." The first of these is open to a number of interpretations; it can mean, for example, poetry written by anyone using the English language who was born in Ireland and lived most or part of his life there. Under this head would come Swift, Tate, Goldsmith, and others—poets who unquestionably belong to English poetry. The second possibility, "Anglo-Irish Poetry," is open to the objection of the limitation of its definition. "Anglo-Irish" means, according to Webster, either persons of English origin or descent living in Ireland, or persons of English and Irish ancestry. No place is left for the native Irishman who learned English and whose descendants knew and spoke English only. It might be pointed out that the numbers of this group increased tremendously during the eighteenth and nineteenth centuries.

We come back, then, to "Irish Poetry"; this term I have used on the precedence of Andrew Malone's *Irish Drama,* John

Cooke's *Dublin Book of Irish Verse*, Stephen Gwynn's *Irish Literature and Drama*, etc., all of which deal with the literature of Ireland written in English. And I have made and used what is a purely arbitrary definition of "Irish Poetry": "Poetry in the English language, written by an Irishman or Anglo-Irishman, and inspired by Ireland or its people." To avoid any confusion with the Irish branch of the Gaelic languages, I have tried to use always the word "Gaelic" in referring to the native tongue, although realizing that "Irish" would be more accurate.

A word as to scope. In Part I, I have not attempted, as I have indicated above, to bring within the bounds of Irish poetry those writers, sometimes called Irish, who have come to be thought of as English. No end is served in calling Swift, for instance, an Irish poet; nor in speaking of him as one of the "origins" of Irish literature.[1] From my point of view, the part played by Swift in Irish literature is an indirect rather than a direct one. I have so indicated in the pages devoted to him. Nor can any juggling with claims and counter-claims bring such men as Goldsmith and Sheridan within the domain of Irish letters. It may be true that when Goldsmith wrote "The Deserted Village" his mind "dwelt lovingly upon his boyhood home."[2] That cannot be proved; the fact remains that Goldsmith in his poetry was English and not Irish. And Sheridan is an integral part of English drama.

The poets and poetry I have discussed fall within the limits of my definition. I have tried to be complete—that is, to discuss, or at least mention all extant Irish poetry—up to 1700. I have not tried to be complete for the period from 1700 to 1798. Irish poetry multiplied rapidly during those years and most of it is pretty dreary. I feel that the writers and examples I have given are enough; certainly enough to justify disagreement with a statement like Stephen Gwynn's that "Irish literature in the English tongue begins with the nineteenth century . . . its be-

[1] Hugh A. Law, *Anglo-Irish Literature*, pp. 14–39.
[2] *Ibid.*, p. 67.

ginnings grew up among, and were formed by, the circumstances which make the years from 1782 to 1800 a turning point
in Irish history." [3]

In Part II, I have tried to keep to my primary aim of showing
how the material of Irish mythology and Gaelic poetry was made
available through translation to the English-speaking people of
Ireland, and how they became interested in, and made use of,
that material.

My thanks are due to Professors Cornelius Weygandt and
Albert C. Baugh for reading and criticizing my manuscript;
and to the authorities of the University of Pennsylvania Library
for their constant and cheerful aid in making available to me
many rare volumes. The publication of this book has been aided
by a grant from the Ella Pancoast Widener Fund authorized by
the Committee on the Publication of Research of the University
of Pennsylvania. Above all, is the obligation to my wife for help
at all times and in all ways in the business of preparation.

R. K. A.

Philadelphia
November 1942

Preface to the Second Edition

I have made only minor changes for the second edition. They
consist of a few stylistic revisions and the addition of several
footnotes.

R. K. A.

West Point, N. Y.
May 1959

[3] Stephen Gwynn, *Irish Literature and Drama,* p. 28.

Contents

Part I

THE POETRY

Introduction

THE term "Irish Poetry" as used in this book means poetry in the English language written by an Irishman or Anglo-Irishman and inspired by Ireland or its people. From the English invasion of 1167 to the eighteenth century, the poetry that would fit such a definition is of slight quantity. This paucity is in great part accounted for by the fact that the English invaders and settlers of Ireland sought not only to conquer the country but also to force an alien tongue upon the inhabitants, something that the Irish stoutly resisted for almost six hundred years. The great mass of the natives continued to use their beloved Gaelic and to follow Gaelic tradition. They knew and recited the songs of their own poets and retold in their own language the exploits of Cuchulin and Finn, of Deirdre and Grania:—songs and stories hidden from the English by the barrier of language. And in the numerous instances in which the two races did mix and become one, it was most often the Englishman who turned Irishman and whose children spoke Gaelic from the cradle. That we may have sufficient background for a study of Irish poetry in these early centuries and understand fully the main reason for the slight quantity of that poetry, we shall glance at the history of the English invasion and the subsequent struggle of the two languages for supremacy.

Gaelic or English?

A WOMAN's impressionableness was the immediate cause for the invasion of Ireland by England. It all began when Dermot MacMurrough, King of Leinster, accompanied Turloch More O'Connor, High King of Ireland, on an invasion of Munster in 1151. During the excitement MacMurrough carried off at her own invitation Dervorgilla, the beautiful wife of Tiernan O'Ruairc, King of Brefni. Growing tired of the lady a little later on, MacMurrough shipped her back to her husband; and we can imagine without too much trouble that the main motive of O'Ruairc's life from this time on was revenge.

His opportunity came in 1166. Murcertach MacLochlann, High King of Ireland after Turloch More O'Connor, was slain in battle; and in the confusion attending the seizure of the high kingship by Rory O'Connor, O'Ruairc invaded Leinster. At the same time the petty chiefs of Leinster revolted; and Dermot MacMurrough, forced to flee, sailed for Bristol on August 1, 1166, to ask help from the English. When in August of the following year he returned with a small force under Richard Fitz-Godebert, the invasion of Ireland by England had started.

A little less than two years later, on May 1, 1169, Maurice Prendergast and Robert FitzStephen, bringing reinforcements of three hundred and ninety men, including thirty knights, landed on the shore of Bannow Bay. On Baginbun headland they built an earthwork, and there is an old Irish rhyme that says,

> At the creeke of Bagganbun
> Ireland was lost and wun! [1]

[1] Quoted by Richard Stanihurst in his "Treatise containing an Plaine and Perfect Description of Ireland," Holinshed's *Chronicles,* London, 1578; rptd., London, 1807, VI, 2.

In 1170 Richard, Earl of Pembroke, nicknamed "Strongbow," came with a thousand men-at-arms. By September of the same year Dublin had fallen. From then on Dublin was to be the English capital of Ireland and the center of the so-called English Pale, or the district within which English influence and power were dominant.

In the course of the next hundred and fifty years, largely because of the vigor of Strongbow and Hugh de Lacy in the center and south of Ireland and of John de Courcy in the north, the English enlarged their holdings to include most of Munster and Connacht, Leinster, Ulster east of Lough Neagh, and Meath. But to a great degree the conquered territories remained alien and hostile, and for many years the English lords and their retainers were forced to remain almost constantly at war or in a state of preparedness for war. Men who spent their waking hours in the saddle and who slept with their weapons at their side had no leisure for the cultivation of letters. But when we discover that, as the English became more firmly established and ordinary life took on a semblance of order bringing with it inevitable communication and exchange of ideas among the English families, there is still very little poetry in English, we must seek for another reason.

That reason is the slow overcoming of the English language by the Gaelic, together with the gradual taking up by the English of native Irish customs. Fynes Moryson says that

About the yeare 1341, the English-Irish (or English Colonies), being degenerated, first began to be enemies of the English . . . [they had] . . . growne barberous by imbracing the tyrannicall Lawes of the Irish . . . which caused them likewise to take Irish names, and to use their language and apparrell.[2]

Curtis has probably best pictured the situation:

In the first century after the Conquest the English race and speech penetrated wide and deep into the country. But . . . the Irish speech

[2] *An Itinerary*. 2nd. ed. II, 167–68.

in the fourteenth century descended again into the plains and reached the town walls. The yeomen and small freeholders, the burgesses of the English towns, as the native race reconquered the soil, steadily forsook the land and emigrated either to England or to the Pale. The great lords of English origin stood their ground, but at the expense of accepting Irish tenants, which they did willingly, and adopting the native speech and civilization.[3]

So strong, in fact, did the native influence become that in 1366 the Statutes of Kilkenny were passed, directed specifically against the

many English . . . [who have forsaken] . . . the English language, fashion, mode of living, laws and usages [and who] live and govern themselves according to the manners, fashion, and language of the Irish enemies, and have . . . made divers marriages and alliances between themselves and the Irish enemies aforesaid; whereby the said land and leige people thereof, the English language, the allegiance due to our Lord the King, and the English laws there, are put in subjection and decayed.[4]

The laws embodied in the Statutes ordered the English to speak English, to follow English customs, and to use English surnames.

But despite vigorous prosecution the Statutes failed to stop the gradual submergence of the English language; and when Poyning's parliament reenacted them in 1495, it ignored the part dealing with the language.

By 1500, [says Curtis] English had lost most of the ground to Irish. . . . By the time of Henry VIII (1509–1547) the true area of English, apart from the towns, was confined to south county Wexford and . . . the Pale—a territory sixty miles long and thirty broad, stretching from Dundalk and Ardee to Kilcullen and the Dublin Mountains. . . . But even in this restricted area Irish was encroaching upon English. A common religious sympathy and resentment at the policy of

---

[3] Edmund Curtis, "The Spoken Languages of Medieval Ireland," *Studies,* VIII (June 1919), 240–41.

[4] Edmund Curtis, *A History of Ireland,* p. 112.

confiscation and persecution which the Tudor government adopted drew together the Irish and the old English, and the symbol of their unity was the Irish language.[5]

Elsewhere Curtis remarks that

So far had the hibernicizing of the once-Norman conquerors and their English tenants gone by Tudor times that in the Dublin parliament which made Henry VIII king of Ireland the Earl of Ormond had to translate the Speaker's address into Irish for the benefit of the Lords and Commons, though they were mainly of old English origin.[6]

The *State Papers, Ireland,* for the sixteenth century have entries time and again referring to the struggle between the two tongues. One of the most striking is that of Lord Chancellor Gerarde in 1587 "to her Majesty's Commissioners. Gerarde affirms that all English, and the most part with delight, even in Dublin, speake Irish, and greatly are spotted in manners, habit and conditions with Irish stains." [7]

Sir John Davies, writing of this same period, makes the accusation that

the English, both Lords and Free-holders, became degenerate and meer Irish in their Language, in their apparrell, in their armes and maner of fight, and all other Customes of life whatsoever. . . . They did not only forget the English Language and scorne the use thereof, but grew to bee ashamed of their very English Names, though they were Noble and of great Antiquity; and tooke Irish *Surnames* and *Nicke-names.*[8]

Stanihurst is rather plaintive about it. He wants to know "whie the English pale is more given to learne the Irish, than the Irishman is willing to learne English." [9] And as late as 1657 the Dublin Assembly Rolls note that

[5] Edmund Curtis, *A History of Medieval Ireland,* p. 243.
[6] *Studies,* VIII, 251.
[7] *State Papers, Ireland, 1574–1585,* p. 130.
[8] *A Discovery of the State of Ireland,* pp. 30, 182.
[9] In Holinshed's *Chronicles,* London, 1808, VI, 6.

There is Irish commonlie and usuallie spoken, and the Irish habitt worn not onelie in the streetes, and by such as live in the countrie and come to the cittie on market days, but alsoe by and in severall families in thie cittie.[10]

Yet looking back now at the struggle between the two languages, we realize that the tide began to turn in 1585 when the forfeited estates of the Earl of Desmond were turned over to the Undertakers (new English settlers who "undertook" to colonize the land). Then came the Ulster Plantation during the reign of James I (1603-1625), and finally the confiscation and "planting" of all Ireland save Connacht and Clare in 1652-54 by Cromwell. Into these two districts of Connacht and Clare the native Irish were huddled; into the remainder of Ireland poured the planters and adventurers from England, delighted with the gift of land and pleased at the prospect of easy living. The situation is well summed up by MacLysaght:

The Conquest of Ireland by Cromwell, completed by William of Orange at the battle of the Boyne, made Ireland into a British Colonial possession; and the end of the seventeenth century, before the English settlers had been long enough in the country to lose any of their sense of being English colonists in a foreign land, was the period when this conception of Ireland's national status was at its height. English families in Ireland regarded it as a place in which they could get a political job or make money in a commercial enterprise.[11]

Inevitably, English began to supplant Irish; Lecky says that in the beginning of the eighteenth century "The Irish tongue over large districts was rapidly disappearing." [12] Corkery puts the native Irish and their language not only beyond "the walls of larger cities . . . but . . . beyond the towns. . . . For Irish Ireland had, by the eighteenth century, become purely a peasant nation." [13] An anonymous letter in *The Gentleman's Magazine*

[10] Jeremiah Hogan, *The English Language in Ireland*, p. 39.

[11] Edward MacLysaght, *Irish Life in the Seventeenth Century: After Cromwell*, p. 135.

[12] W. E. H. Lecky, *A History of Ireland in the Eighteenth Century*, I, 331.

[13] Daniel Corkery, *The Hidden Ireland*, p. 7.

for October 1751, bears witness to the truth of Corkery's statement. The writer spent a summer in the remote country parts of Ireland, where, he said, "the lower rank have as yet received scarce any tincture of the manners, habit, customs, or language of Britain." [14]

And during these years the English Government was making vigorous and ceaseless efforts to stamp out the Gaelic tongue; and, of course, religion enters the picture. The charter of the Incorporated Society for Promoting English Protestant Schools in Ireland, granted by George II in 1733, reads in part, "To the intent therefore that the Children of the Popish, and other poor Natives of the said Kingdom may be instructed in the English Tongue. . . ." [15] And Thomas, Lord Bishop of Oxford, in a sermon preached in 1757, mentions one fact of

great Extent and Importance; which would God were observed in this Nation (Ireland), combining Instruction with Labour. The first of Instruction, to such as need it, is teaching them *English:* for till they understand that competently, their only Inlet of Knowledge is from the Priests and their followers. [16]

So successful were the efforts of Church and State that by the beginning of the nineteenth century the Gaelic language had pretty well disappeared from Ireland save in the far parts of the country districts.

Conditions for a literature in English in Ireland, then, were increasingly favorable from the late seventeenth and early eighteenth centuries on. Such a literature did develop, but we can speak of only a small part of it as Irish literature. Many of the Irish writers of these years who wrote in English—such men as Goldsmith and Sheridan—seemed hardly aware of the country they had been born in. Was it not, after all, the habitat of the

[14] XXI, 466.

[15] An abstract of the charter is on pp. 15–16 of *A Sermon preached at Christ-Church, Dublin, 27th June 1762 before the . . . Society . . .* , Dublin, 1762.

[16] *A Sermon Preached before the Society . . .* , by Thomas, Lord Bishop of Oxford, London, 1757, p. 17.

"meer Irish," and did not one find in the England of the day all that the heart and mind wanted? And when an Irish poet did treat of the Irish scene or of Irish people, and hence wrote what can rightfully be called "Irish poetry," in all but a few cases he put into his work no distinctive quality of rhythm, diction, or subject matter that would have definitely labeled it "Irish." The following quatrain, for instance, is quoted by John Dunton, who, traveling in Ireland in 1699, mentions it in a letter to a friend as a piece of what he calls "Irish poetry." He found it inscribed upon Lord Taragh's tombstone in St. James Churchyard in Dublin:

> The Generous and Illustrious Thomas Preston
> Lord Viscount of Taragh lyes under this stone
> In the prime of his youth about twenty and one
> This hopefull blossom was cropped and gone.[17]

Joseph Ritson, in the preface to his *Select Collection of English Songs* (1783), gives a clear picture of what an English critic of Ritson's day thought of Irish poetry:

With respect to the lyric productions of our now sister-kingdom Ireland, the best of them have been generally esteemed and ranked as English songs, being few in number, and possessing no national, or other peculiar or distinguishing marks; of these, however, the number is very few.[18]

He amplifies this criticism in a note that shows also the eighteenth-century Englishman's conception of the native Irish:

The distinction between English and Scottish songs . . . arises—not from the language in which they are written, for that may be common to both, but—from the country to which they respectively belong, or of which their authors are natives. This discrimination does not so necessarily or properly apply to Ireland; great part of which was colonised from this kingdom, and the descendants of the settlers, the only civilized and cultivated inhabitants, have consequently, been,

[17] MacLysaght, *op. cit.,* Appendix B, p. 326, from MS. Rawl. D 71.
[18] I, vii.

ever since, looked upon as English. . . . Everyone has heard of the English Pale.[19]

But despite this worshipping of things English by the vast majority of the Anglo-Irish, an increasing number of them during the seventeenth and eighteenth centuries began to grow aware of a large body of native legend and story as it was made available to them through translation. They learned the stories of the Red Branch and the Fianna; they found that the despised Irish were really people and, moreover, people who had as their inheritance myths and legends as romantic and lovely as the stories of Lancelot, of Roland, or of Siegfried. And for the first time, as it were, they looked about them, and they found this pleasant green island teeming with superstition and old story: hardly a cave or a rock or a stream but had its legend that came out of remote time. They began to listen to the queer idiom that the native Irish, who had learned English during their lifetime, used when they tried to bend the thoughts of their race into the new tongue. When the Irish poets began to use in their poetry this matter of Ireland: the myths, the legends, the superstitions, the countryside; and when they expressed themselves in rhythms different from the rhythms of English poetry: rhythms they learned by listening to the speech of the peasants, then Irish poetry took on distinction of meaning.

Such distinction is not evident until the early nineteenth century. But Irish poetry was written, though at first apparently in very slight quantity, from almost the beginning of the English occupation; and our task here is a consideration of that poetry up to the '98 "troubles." Immediately, we are concerned with the period from 1167 to 1400.

[19] *Ibid.*, I, vii, *n.*

✣ 3 ✣

From the Invasion to 1400

SINCE the English lords and their retainers were occupied for a number of years after the invasion in keeping their domains subdued; and since, when a measure of quiet had been brought about, their language largely gave way to Gaelic, we must look elsewhere for poetry in English, at least in the first part of this period.

One of the laws of the Kilkenny Statutes directed that only Englishmen were to be admitted to benefices, abbeys, and cathedrals. This law was a reaffirmation of one passed by the Kilkenny parliament of 1310, which said that no *merus hibernicus* (mere Irishman) could be a member of a religious order in that part of the country under English lordship. Because a law of this type, unlike one against the use of the Gaelic language, could be administered with comparative ease, it was probably for the most part obeyed; and as monasteries and abbeys meant in the main quiet and leisure, it follows that we should look for the earliest Irish poetry to come from a religious house.

Such, indeed, seems to be the case. In the monastery that the Franciscans, or Grey Friars, founded at Kildare sometime between 1260 and 1277,[20] a manuscript of prose and verse in English, French, and Latin was written in the early fourteenth century. The manuscript has survived and is known today as number 913 of the Harley collection in the British Museum. It is described by Wanley, in the *Bibliothecae Harleianae,* as "A parchment Book in 12mo, written partly in English, and partly in Latin by divers hands." Although much of the material in the manuscript was probably only copied in the Kildare abbey, some of it was undoubtedly composed there.

[20] E. B. Fitzmaurice and A. G. Little, *Materials for the History of the Franciscan Province of Ireland 1230–1450,* pp. 44–45.

The reasons for assigning the manuscript to Kildare have been discussed by Croker, Heuser, and Seymour.[21] The most important are the stated authorship of one of the religious poems in these lines:

> This song wroght a frere
> Jesus Christ be is socure
> Louerd, bring him to the toure,
> Frere Michel Kyldare . . . ;[22]

the fact that there is a ballad on the death of Piers de Bermingham who was buried at Kildare in 1308;[23] and local allusions in the poem "The Land of Cokaygne."

The subsequent history of the manuscript, after its composition, is interesting. Some time after 1543 when Henry VIII granted the Franciscan abbey at Kildare, along with other properties, to "Daniel Sutton, at the annual rent of 2s. 3d. Irish money,"[24] the manuscript came into the possession of George Wyse, bailiff of Waterford in 1566 and mayor in 1571. This fact we know because Wyse's name is on one of the pages as owner. We next hear of it in 1608 as "The Book of Rosse or of Waterford" in a mention in MS 418, Lansdowne, a collection made for Sir James Ware that contains several pieces from our manuscript. In 1697 it is mentioned in Bernard's *Catalogi librorum manuscriptorum Angliae et Hiberniae* as being in the library of Bishop Moore. From him it passed to Bishop Tanner, then to the Earl of Oxford, and finally to the British Museum.[25]

Of particular concern to us are the poems in English in the manuscript that give evidence of Irish authorship. The first of these, Friar Michael's poem "Sweet Iesus," is the best of the

---

[21] Crofton Croker, ed., *Popular Songs of Ireland*, pp. 262–71; W. Heuser, *Die Kildare-Gedichte*, pp. 1–19; St. John Seymour, *Anglo-Irish Literature 1200–1582*, pp. 5–6.

[22] Heuser, *op. cit.*, p. 85.

[23] Fitzmaurice and Little, *op. cit.*, pp. 88–89.

[24] Mervyn Archdall, *Monasticon Hibernicum*, p. 331.

[25] Croker, *op. cit.*, pp. 267–71; Heuser, *op. cit.*, pp. 3–4; Seymour, *op. cit.*, pp. 4–7.

religious pieces. Despite the didacticism of the verse, its rude vigor and simplicity fix it in the memory:

> This world is loue is gon awai
> So dew on grasse in somer is dai,
> Few ther beth, weilawai,
> That louith goddis lore.[26]
>
> . . .
>
> Pouir was thin incomming,
> So ssal be thin outegoing,
> Thou ne ssalt of al thi thing
> A peni ber to molde.[27]

Nothing so good as these lines is in the remaining religious pieces. "A Sermon," "Fifteen Signs of the Day of Judgment," "The Fall and Passion," "The Ten Commandments," "The Seven Sins," and "Christ on the Cross," all of which were possibly also composed by Friar Michael,[28] hardly rise above the general level of Middle English religious verse. But the secular pieces have among them a number that merit consideration.

The best is the unique copy of "The Land of Cokaygne," that Frederick James Furnivall called "the airiest and cleverest piece of satire in the whole range of Early English, if not of English, poetry." [29] It was first discussed adequately by Thomas Wright in his *Saint Patrick's Purgatory,* along with other poems of the Middle Ages that treat of "Cocaigne," or "cookery," land.[30]

Whether or not the satirist had Kildare in mind as the land of the friendly religious houses that he tells about in his poem cannot be said definitely, but it is possible he did. At three places in the poem occur what might be local allusions:

---

[26] Heuser, *op. cit.,* p. 81.

[27] *Ibid.,* p. 82.

[28] Seymour, *op. cit.,* pp. 57–76.

[29] *Early English Poems and Lives of Saints,* Berlin, 1886, p. 331.

[30] London, 1844, pp. 53–59. Wright also mentions something, *n.,* p. 53, of the history of Harley 913.

> Ther is a wel fair abbei
> Of white monkes and of grei [31]
>
> An other abbei is ther bi,
> For soth a gret fair nunnerie [32]
>
> And snellich berrith forth har prei
> To the mochil grei abbei.[33]

Kildare was the home of at least three religious institutions. First, there was the great double monastery founded by St. Brigit about 484, where monks and nuns lived in the same building separated only by a wall. Second, there was the monastery of the Franciscans, called Grey Abbey, "on the south side of town," [34] founded between 1260 and 1277 by William de Vescy and Gerald FitzMaurice, Lord Offaly.[35] Third, there was the house of the Carmelites, or White Friars, founded in 1290 by William de Vescy, presumably somewhat close to Grey Abbey, for both Grey Abbey and the house of the White Friars were granted to Daniel Sutton at the dissolution of the monasteries.[36] If we can say that "a wel fair abbei Of white monkes and of grei" refers to two abbeys—an abbey of white monks and an abbey of grey monks—then the Franciscan and Carmelite houses fit the allusion.

"A gret fair nunnerie" is perhaps St. Brigit's double monastery that lasted, according to Archdall, until the reign of Elizabeth, who granted it to Anthony Deeringe.[37] It was more than likely to be called "gret" because the church was "of unusual size"; [38] and it would be called a nunnery rather than a

---

[31] Heuser, *op. cit.*, p. 146.
[32] *Ibid.*, p. 149.
[33] *Ibid.*
[34] Archdall, *op. cit.*, p. 330.
[35] Fitzmaurice and Little, *op. cit.*, pp. 44–45.
[36] Archdall, *op. cit.*, p. 331.
[37] *Ibid.*, p. 323.
[38] James F. Kenney, *The Sources for the Early History of Ireland*, I, 356.

monastery because "Tradition and custom alike . . . assigned the predominant position to Brigit and the abbesses who succeeded her: according to some accounts, the abbot of the men's community was appointed by the abbess." [39] Apparently the author of "The Land of Cokaygne" had a double monastery in mind, for much of the satire of the piece rests on the fact of monks and nuns living close together.

If we add to these suppositions the evidence of the poem's being in a manuscript that was written in the Franciscan monastery at Kildare, it would seem that Cokaygne land can be identified with Kildare. And linguistic characteristics in the poem point to its Irish composition.[40]

The poem merits Furnivall's praise. In that country of the "gilofre of gode smakke" and of "Throstle, thruisse, and nightingale," the young nuns and youthful monks spend the time very pleasantly indeed. The impudence of the satire is so engaging that we do not particularly care if the actual monastic conditions were such that they give the satire point; we are content to read and smile. Nor should the description in the poem be overlooked: flowers and birds of all kinds make happy the long days in Cokaygne, and the medieval love of color shows in the green jasper and red coral of the cloister pillars, as well as in the strange riot of precious stones and gold that form the beds of the streams:

> Of thai stremis al the molde:
> Stonis preciuse and golde.
> Ther is saphir and vniune,
> Carbuncle and astiune,
> Smaragde, lugre and prassiune,
> Beril, onix, topasiune,
> Ametist and crisolite,
> Calcedun and epetite.[41]

[39] James F. Kenney, *The Sources for the Early History of Ireland*, I, 356.
[40] Heuser, *op. cit.*, pp. 141–45.
[41] *Ibid.*, p. 147.

Excellent poet that the author of "The Land of Cokaygne" was, he is very nearly equaled by the high-spirited goliard who wrote the poem sometimes called "A Satire on the People of Kildare," another of the secular pieces in Harley 913, and again, because of distinguishing features of language, very probably written in Ireland. And here we come on one of the very few early poems that has in it anything we might term "distinctively" Irish. For as Irish as James Stephens's *The Crock of Gold* and *The Demi-Gods* are the fun and irreverence with which angels, archangels, saints, and the members of the Trinity itself, as well as brewers, bakers, cobblers, skinners, and other tradesmen, are treated. Because of the five monastic orders satirized Heuser suggests that the poem, although found in the Kildare manuscript, is aimed at Dublin and its inhabitants rather than at Kildare and its people.[42] We might add that the teeming life of trade of a town the size of Dublin would have been more likely to remain impressed on the mind of a traveler than would the trade life of a smaller town like Kildare. If the poem is the work of a goliard—those wandering students of the Middle Ages who served as jesters or minstrels—surely his journeyings took him to Dublin, then as now the center of Irish life.

No one escapes the pungent wit of the satirist. Here is the stanza to St. Christopher and the stanza to the brewers:

> Hail seint Christofre with thi lang stake!
> Thou ber ur louerd Iesus Crist ouer the brod lake,
> Mani grete kunger swimmeth abute thi fete.
> Hou mani hering to peni at West Chep in London?
> This uers is of holi writte,
> Hit com of noble witte.[43]
> Hail be ye brewesters with yur galuns,
> Potels and quartes ouer al the tounes.
> Yur thowmes berrith moch awai, schame hab the gyle;
> Beth iwar of the coking-stole, the lak is dep and hori.

[42] *Ibid.*, pp. 150–54.
[43] *Ibid.*, p. 155.

> Sikerlich he was a clerk
> That so sleilich wroughte this werk.[44]

The other eighteen stanzas discuss in a similar way St. Michael, St. Dominic, St. Francis, St. Mary; the friars, monks, nuns, gilmins, priests; the merchants, tailors, cobblers, skinners, potters, bakers, hucksters, caitiffs; and Christ. Over the whole poem flashes and sparkles a sunny malice that laughs at and with everything, including itself.

Helping to fix the time and place of the composition of Harley 913 is the ballad on the death of Piers de Bermingham, who, as mentioned above, was buried at Kildare in 1308. Local allusions and the dialect indicate Irish authorship. Piers, Baron of Tethmoy in Offaly, was one of the most ruthless of the early invaders of Ireland; he capped his career by the murder of the O'Conors, kings of Ui Failghe, while they were his guests at a feast of the Holy Trinity.[45] For this pleasant piece of work he was widely praised, and the writer of the ballad on his death sees nothing untoward in any of his actions. Piers is extolled specifically for his merciless hunting out of the native Irish:

> An other thing al so:
> To yrismen he was fo,
> That wel wide whare.
> Euer he rode aboute
> With streinth to hunt ham vte,
> As hunter doth the hare.[46]

The ballad is twenty-two stanzas long and the poetry of all of it is as mediocre as the quotation indicates.

Probably a little later in composition than the poems mentioned, although in the same manuscript, is "A Song on the Times," dealing with the evils and corruptions of rich and poor, and supposedly of Irish origin.[47] It is not a very good poem; the

[44] Heuser, *op. cit.,* p. 157.
[45] Curtis, *A History of Medieval Ireland,* p. 226.
[46] Heuser, *op. cit.,* p. 162.
[47] Seymour, *op. cit.,* p. 81.

author is heavy-handed in his moralizing and does not have
the simple directness of Friar Michael. We can easily imagine
him to have been a reformer, lifting his hands in horror at what
his gimlet eyes saw. A fair sample of the twenty-five eight-line
complaining stanzas is the first:

> Whose thenchith vp this carful lif,
> Nighte and dai that we beth inne,
> So moch we seeth of sorow and strif,
> And lite ther is of world is winne;
> Hate and wreth ther is wel riue,
> And trew loue is ful thinne;
> Men that beth in heiighist liue
> Mest icharged beth with sinne.[48]

Of the other English poems, or poems in English, in the
manuscript—"Elde," [49] "Erthe," [50] "Lullaby," [51] "Five Evil
Things," [52] "Nego," [53] and "A Rhyme-Beginning Fragment" [54]
—only the last-named, because of its dialectal peculiarities, can
be said with any certainty to be Irish. The others were probably
only copied in Ireland. "A Rhyme-Beginning Fragment" is a
curious little philosophical piece. Since it is short, I quote it in
full:

> Loue hauith me broght in lithir thoght,
> 　Thoght ich ab to blinne;
> Blinne to thench hit is for noght,
> 　Noght is loue of sinne.
>
> Sinne me hauith in care ibroght,
> 　Broght in mochil vnwinne;
> Winne to weld ich had ithoght;
> 　Thoght is that ich am inne.

[48] Heuser, op. cit., p. 133.
[49] Ibid., pp. 167–72.
[50] Ibid., pp. 176–83.
[51] Ibid., pp. 172–76.
[52] Ibid., pp. 183–84.
[53] Ibid., pp. 139–40.
[54] Ibid., pp. 165–66.

In me is care, how I ssal fare,
Fare ich wol and funde;
Funde ich with outen are,
Ar i be broght to grunde.[55]

Besides the pieces in Harley 913, extant poems written in
English in the Ireland of these early years after the occupation
are scarce. Two poems published in *Reliquiae Antiquae,* "A
Poem on Blood-Letting" and "A Fragment of a Poem on the
Virtues of Herbs," [56] are discussed by Heuser [57] who concludes
they are of Irish origin because of their dialect. Thomas Wright
took these poems for his *Reliquiae Antiquae* from a duodecimo
volume of the late fourteenth century owned by C. W. Loscombe. Because "The Virtue of Herbs" is a fragment, Heuser
attempted to trace the manuscript in order to make a full transcript. He found that it was sold in 1854 to Lord Ashburnham
and was bought on May 1, 1899, by Leighton, the London bookseller. Heuser could trace the manuscript no further.

Recently, however, among the Croker manuscripts in the
British Museum, a transcript of sixty-eight of the remaining
lines of "The Virtues of Herbs" and a transcript of a fifteenth-
century version of the same poem, 195 lines long, have been
found. Both of these were made by Thomas Wright and sent
to Crofton Croker, probably for a projected work of Croker's
on Irish poetry. Both transcripts contain the lines,

All of the herbys of Ierlonde
Here thou schalt know everi onde.

This couplet and the fact of Wright's sending the poems to
Croker, a known Irish antiquary, apparently bear out Heuser's
conclusions that the poems are Irish.[58] Neither poem is of any
particular worth.

[55] Heuser, *p.* 166.
[56] I, 189–91; I, 194–97.
[57] *Op. cit.,* pp. 71–75.
[58] P. J. Irwin, "The Lost Loscombe Mss.: A Transcript," *Anglia,* LVII (Sept.
1933), pp. 397–400.

The poems in Harley 913 and in the Loscombe manuscript
are probably the earliest verse in English of which it can be said
with reasonable certainty that it was written in Ireland. But in
the latest catalogue of the Lambeth Palace manuscripts there
are printed two stanzas of verse which, if definitely proved to be
of Irish origin, perhaps antedate, or are at least as early as, the
Kildare and Loscombe pieces.[59] The description of the manuscript in which the verses appear reads:

Cent. xiii late, in a small, rather difficult hand, somewhat of charter
type: much contracted. . . . A memorandum at the end shows that
the book was in Ireland (Cashel) in century xv. It was probably com-
piled by an Irish friar (or monk) and may have come via Lanthony.

A large number of the *Codices Lambethani,* among which is
the manuscript just mentioned, came from the Augustinian
priory of Lanthony near Gloucester. This Lanthony was at first
a cell to the original house that was founded at Lanthony in
Monmouthshire in 1108 and endowed by Hugh de Lacy.[60] Because of the poverty of the place and the rudeness of the people,
most of the canons removed to a site near Gloucester in 1136 and
formed a monastery that came to be called Lanthony the second; and by the time of the reign of Henry VIII the first Lanthony was a cell to the second.[61] Constant communication and
travel took place between the two houses.

Of especial interest are the endowment by Hugh de Lacy or
the first Lanthony and further endowments by Walter and Gilbert de Lacy.[62] This Hugh de Lacy was the one who came to
Ireland in 1171 with Henry II, and was made warden of Dublin
and justiciar of Ireland. Hence a relationship between Ireland
and Lanthony the first is easily established.[63] Additional evi-

[59] M. R. James and Claude Jenkins, *A Descriptive Catalogue of the Manuscripts in the Library of Lambeth Palace,* #557, f. 6, 185b.

[60] Sir William Dugdale, *Monasticon Anglicanum,* VI, 569–70.

[61] *Ibid.*

[62] *Ibid.*

[63] Clark Harris Slover, "Early Literary Channels between Great Britain and
Ireland," *University of Texas Studies in English,* No. 6, December 1926, pp.

dence of communication of a well-defined sort between the two places is the fact that the Abbey of Great Conall in the County of Kildare, a cell to the Abbey of Lanthony the first, was founded in 1202 and filled by the founder with canons regular from Lanthony the first.[64] Although Hugh de Lacy was murdered in 1186 and the last of the direct line of his descendants died about the middle of the fourteenth century, there were collateral branches of the family that continued to wield influence in Ireland very nearly to the present.[65] In view of these facts, then, it was quite possible for manuscripts to be brought from Ireland during the Middle Ages to either the first or second Lanthony.

Since the stanzas apparently have not been noticed elsewhere, I give them in full:

Allas allas vel yuel y sped
for synne Jesu fro me ys fled yat lyuely frere
At my dore he standeth at one
And kallys undo yit reuful mone on yis mannere
Undo my lef my downe dere
Undo my stond stekyn out here I yk (?) am yi make
Lo my heued and myne lockys
Ar al by weuyd wyt blody dropys for yine sake

Alle yat gos and rydys loket op on me
If euere seye ye pynyn man al so men pynen me
Loke man to my backe hou yt ys betyn
Loke to my sydyn wat blod it hauyn iletyn
Loke doune to myne fet yat nayled been on rode
Loke to myn heuyd yat rennyn al on blode
to clensyn ye of synne op on ye rode tre
I suffrede all yus pyn man for loue of ye
Gyf you me yat soule yat ys so dere y bouyhte
Of all yat I yole ne ys me yen nouyhte.

5-52; No. 7, November 1927, pp. 5-11, shows constant communication up to 1170 between the monasteries of the two countries.

[64] Dugdale, *op. cit.*, VII, 1138.
[65] Curtis, *A History of Medieval Ireland*, pp. 247-48.

From the thirteenth and fourteenth centuries remain only a one-stanza song, perhaps incomplete; a number of fragments scattered through the Red Book of Ossory that were jotted down by Bishop de Ledrede, Bishop of Ossory from about 1316 to 1360; and a single stanza of a fourteenth-century poem addressed to the young men of Waterford.

The one-stanza song, said by Wells to be "perhaps the earliest English dance-song extant" [66] and dated by him 1300–1350, is in manuscript Rawlinson D. 913. Although probably sung by an Irish girl, the Irish origin of the song remains doubtful despite Mr. Seymour's remark that "it is placed in the mouth of an Anglo-Irish girl, and so presumably was composed by an Anglo-Irish minstrel." [67] Dialectically it is of the south of England.[68] The few lines have a freshness and charm that are not elsewhere in the early poetry:

> Icham of Irlaunde
> Ant of the holy londe of irlande
> Gode sir pray ich ye
> for of saynte charite,
> come ant daunce wyt me,
> in irlaunde.[69]

When a friend repeated this stanza to W. B. Yeats, he used it as the basis for a five-stanza poem, "I am of Ireland," published first in *Words for Music, Perhaps and Other Poems* (1932). The lines that follow, used for three of these stanzas—thus forming an interesting use of the refrain—are the lines that come directly from the earlier poem.

> 'I am of Ireland,
> And the Holy Land of Ireland,

[66] John E. Wells, *A Manual of the Writings in Middle English 1050–1400*, p. 493.

[67] *Op. cit.*, p. 98.

[68] W. Heuser, "Fragments von unbekannten Spielmannsliedern des 14 Jahrhunderts aus Ms. Rawl. D. 913," *Anglia*, XXX (1907), pp. 173 ff.

[69] *Ibid.*, p. 175.

And time runs on,' cried she.
'Come out of charity,
Come dance with me in Ireland.' [70]

The fragments in the Red Book of Ossory are the remains of
what was undoubtedly a popular oral literature of fourteenth-
century Kilkenny. Most are of one or two lines only; for instance,

Hey how the cheualdoures wok al nyght [71]

and

So do nightyngale synge ful myrie
Shal y neure for thyn loue lengre karie.[72]

The longest is four lines; part of a ballad, probably, that told of
a girl's troublous marriage with a much older man:

Alas, hou shold y syng yloren is my playing
Hou shold y with that olde man
To leven and (*oblit*.) my leman
Swettist of al thinge.[73]

The single stanza addressed to the young men of Waterford
is the beginning of a longer fourteenth-century poem that was
copied in 1608 into manuscript Lansdowne 418 from Harley 913
when the latter was larger than it is now. The transcript was
made for Sir James Ware, and the scribe who was doing the
copying for him from Harley 913 wrote the following note
about the poem:

There is in this book [Harley 913] a long discourse in meter putting
the youth of Waterford in mind of harme taken by the povers, and
wishing them to beware for the time to come; I have written out the
first staffe only.[74]

[70] *Collected Poems*, p. 306.
[71] *Historical Manuscripts Commission*, Vol. 14, 10th report, appendix, pt. V,
p. 248.
[72] *Ibid.*, p. 247.
[73] *Ibid.*, p. 244.
[74] *A Catalogue of the Lansdowne Manuscripts in the British Museum*, MS
418, #37, p. 118.

The warning is apparently against the Poers, or Powers, a great Anglo-Norman family living near Waterford:

> Yung men of Waterford lernith now to plei
> For yur mere is plowis i lad beth a wey
> Scur ye yur hanfelis yt lang habith i lei
> And fend you of the pouers that waltith by the wey
> > Ich rede
> For if hi takith you on and on
> fram ham scapith ther never one
> I swar bi Christ and St. Jon
> > That of goth yur hede.[75]

From the time of the writing of these scattered pieces until late in the fifteenth century there is extant, apparently, no other Irish poetry.

[75] Heuser, *Die Kildare-Gedichte*, p. 11; Seymour, *op. cit.*, p. 88.

The Fifteenth and Sixteenth Centuries

DURING these centuries the volume of extant Irish poetry increases somewhat. Besides miscellaneous verse, that includes the pieces in the Hanmer collection and in the *Book of Howth*, there is the work of Richard Stanihurst, the first Irish poet of whom we have any definite knowledge.

The miscellaneous verse begins with two poems on Waterford, printed by Croker in his *Popular Songs of Ireland*. The manuscript volume out of which Croker dug the poems "appears," he says, "to be the collection of some laborious antiquary about the latter end of the reign of Elizabeth." [76] That manuscript volume is known now as the "Hanmer Papers" and is printed in the Addenda of the *State Papers, Ireland, 1601–1603*. The collector of these papers, Meredith Hanmer, D.D. (1543–1604), a Shropshire Englishman, best known for his *Chronicle of Ireland* that was published by Sir James Ware in 1633, spent the years from 1591 to his death in 1604 in Ireland.[77] The time he had left from his duties in the church—and it must have been considerable—he seems to have devoted to research into the antiquities of Ireland,[78] and his papers have in them much of interest besides the two poems noticed by Croker.

The earlier of the two poems, "The Mayor of Waterford's Letter," written in or a little after the year 1487, concerns the attempt of the Earl of Kildare and the Anglo-Irish lords to have Lambert Simnel crowned Edward VI of Ireland and England. On May 24, 1487, Simnel was actually crowned in St. Mary's

---

[76] Croker, *op. cit.,* p. 293.

[77] *DNB.*

[78] He wrote to Burghley March 23, 1593–94 (*State Papers, Ireland,* V, 229) about the unsettled state in Ireland and Tirone's power, ending, "I beinge sett a worke to collect the antiquities of this land and to registre them unto the posteritie, doe come to the knowledge and view of these things."

Church in Dublin; and all Ireland accepted him save Waterford
and a few other towns. An appeal was made to Waterford to
join in the recognition; the town refused, and shortly afterward
the mayor of Waterford addressed a long metrical epistle to the

> . . . most noble pastour, chosen of God,
> Walter, Archbishop of Dublin,

which in the course of its forty-four doggerel stanzas sorrows for
the present unhappy relations between Waterford and Dublin,
asks Dublin to repent for its part in the rebellion, and proves
Henry VII's right to the throne.[79]

The second, and later, of the two poems, "The Praise of
Waterford," dated by internal evidence about 1545 and perhaps
composed by Patrick Strong whose name appears at the head of
the poem as town clerk, recites in twenty-two stanzas of what
again is only doggerel the privileges granted Waterford by the
English kings in return for the city's loyalty.[80] The first stanza
is a fair specimen of all twenty-two:

> God of his goodness, praysed that he be,
>> For the daylie increase of thy good fame;
> O pleasant Waterford, thow loyall cytie,
>> That five hundred yeres receavest thy name
> Er the later conquest unto thee came;
>> In Ireland deservest to be peerless—
> *Quia tu semper intacta manes.*

Possibly Croker did not think the other poetry in the Hanmer
papers of sufficient interest to print; or it may be that it was not
available to him, since when he examined the Hanmer volume
many of the pages were "pasted over with apparently unar-
ranged scraps and memoranda."[81] Of most interest in this other
poetry is the earliest translation of an Irish song into English
that I know of. The entry in the *State Papers* reads:

[79] Croker, *op. cit.*, pp. 293–312.
[80] *Ibid.*, pp. 312–20.
[81] *Ibid.*, p. 293.

An Irish song, interlined with English translation, as follows:

You and I will go to Finegall.
You and I will eat such meats as we find there.
You and I will steal such beef as we find fat
I shall be hanged and you shall be hanged. What shall our children
    do?
When teeth do grow unto themselves as their fathers did before? [82]

This translation is probably of a street song; the reference of
going to Finegal, or the English Pale, and committing thievery
that would bring hanging at the hands of the English points
rather clearly to popular origin. Likewise, the need for stealing
meat from the inhabitants of the Pale would seem a reflection
of the starving plight of the poorer classes of the native Irish
during the Elizabethan wars.

We do not know whether Hanmer himself was the translator
of the song; we do not know whether he knew Irish although
he lists twenty-eight Irish words, with their meanings, in his
Chronicle of Ireland.[83] Nor can we tell definitely if he was the
author of the following poems in English listed by the *State
Papers* as being in the "Hanmer Papers," though presumably he
was. Here is the list:

Fragments of verse on Irish manners.	p. 1 (small)
Ribald rhyme denouncing Roman Catholic friars, nuns, and canons, and rejoicing at the downfall of the abbeys.	p. ½
Verses prophetic of English history.	p. 3
Verses as before prophetic of English hist.?	p. 5, with fragment

Verses on the history of France (?). These are in the *State
Papers,* and I quote them in full:

> The state of France as there it stands
> Is like primire at my hands.

[82] *Calendar of the State Papers Relating to Ireland, 1601–1603*, Addenda, pp.
681–82.
[83] Sir James Ware, ed., *Ancient Irish Histories*, 1809, II, 21–23.

Some do vie and some do hold.
The best assured may be bold.
The King was rash without regard
And being fluch would needs discard.
And first he post it to the goyes,
And of nowght (?) straightway it vies.
Queen mother standing at the back
And taught them all to make the pack;
And we that saw them at their play
Left them there and came our way.

Postscript:—

The Lords do crave all;
The King accords all;
The Parliament passeth all;
The Chancellor doth seal (?) all;
Queen Mother doth rule all;
The Cardinals do bless all;
The Pope doth pardon all;
And, without God's help, the divill will have all.[84]

p. ½

Probably during the same years that Dr. Hanmer was delving into Irish antiquities, the *Book of Howth* was written. This small folio volume, done on sixteenth century vellum in thirteen different hands, belonged originally to the Howth family, found its way into the archives of Dublin castle, then came into the possession of Carew, and is now in the library at Lambeth.[85] Curtis, who says it is based on Cambrensis and a Latin book once in the hands of the O'Neills,[86] has aptly styled it the *chanson de geste* of John de Courcy, the conqueror of Ulster. Although the *Book of Howth* contains much Irish tradition and history, it unfortunately has but one poem. Seymour, strangely

[84] Pp. 684–85.

[85] Published in the *Calendar of the Carew Manuscripts,* London, 1871, V, 1–260. For an account of the MS of the *Book of Howth,* see the introduction to Vol. V.

[86] *Studies,* VIII, 250.

enough, speaks of two poems; one of these, a seven-line piece beginning "Deceit deceiveth and shall be deceived," he says is on page 84 of the *Book of Howth* as published in Volume V of the *Calendar of the Carew Manuscripts*. But the seven lines Seymour quotes are from Lydgate's "Fall of Princes." [87]

The only poem in the *Book of Howth* is a sixteen-stanza piece on the Templars, particularizing the life of the last Grand Master, Jacques de Molay, "who," says Seymour, "was put to death by Philip le Bel, King of France. It seems improbable, therefore, that this poem comes from the pen of an Anglo-Irish writer." [88] This statement seems curious in the light of certain facts. First, the entry in the *Book of Howth* immediately following the poem and in the same handwriting shows interest in the Templars of Ireland only. Here it is:

All the possessions of these Templars were given unto the religion of Knights of St. John the Baptist. They were convicted in ten articles of heresy, not fruitful to be put in memory, A.D. 1311. In Ireland their houses was Clone-tarf, Donebrowe, Gormanstoune, Kilmaynam by Kelles, Palmerstoune, and divers other, & c.[89]

Second, there are seven other entries about the Templars in the *Book of Howth*.[90] Third, the burning of Jacques de Molay in 1314, two years after the final suppression of the order, marked the utter extermination of the once proudest and wealthiest knights in Christendom, and surely interested the Irish and Anglo-Irish as well as the rest of Europe. For these reasons it seems to me that there is more likelihood of the author's being Irish than not. The poem itself is of little worth, as the first stanza shows:

> Chroniclers the truth can record,
> Calling to mind the first foundation,

[87] Seymour, *op. cit.*, pp. 99–100. The lines are 4432–38 of Part I of the *Fall of Princes* as edited by Henry Bergen for the Carnegie Institute of Washington, D.C., 1923, Publication #262.

[88] *Op. cit.*, p. 100.

[89] *Carew MSS*, V, 237.

[90] Pp. 129, 131, 169, 239, 325, 334, 429.

> And old authors there with all accord,
> Of these Templars the religious gan
> That time when Godfrey Bullion had wan,
> That noble knightly man,
> Hierusalem, that Order first began.[91]

But if the poetry in the *Book of Howth* is worth little, the prose makes up for it; the stories of legend and history that abound therein,[91a] as well as the saga of John de Courcy, are of primary importance.

Among the miscellaneous material in the Carew manuscripts are six lines of poetry that apparently were written by an Anglo-Irishman who was in despair at the way in which the English language and customs were being overcome by the Irish. Since the lines were written originally in the White Book of the Exchequer of Dublin the conditions they speak of evidently were common in the Pale itself:

> By graunting charters of peace
> To falce Englishe wtouen lesse,
> This land shall be much undo.
> But gossiprede and alterage,
> And lessinge of our languadge,
> Have micklie holp theretoo.[92]

These lines, as well as practically all the other poetry we have so far considered, are anonymous; the only poet we have been able to name with any degree of certainty is Friar Michael of Kildare. But in the latter part of the sixteenth century and the first years of the seventeenth, there lived an Irish poet, Richard Stanihurst (1547–1618), of whom we know comparatively a good deal. He was born in Dublin, the son of James Stanihurst who was recorder of Dublin and speaker of the Irish House of Commons in the parliaments of 1557, 1560, and 1568. Richard attended the famous school of Peter White at Kilkenny and from there went to Oxford. After graduation he studied law in Lon-

[91] *Carew MSS*, V, 234.
[91a] See below, pp. 63-67.
[92] *Ibid.*, p. 452.

don for a time; then returned to Ireland, accompanied by
Edmund Campion as his tutor, where he wrote a *Description
of Ireland* and a *History of Ireland during the Reign of Henry
VIII* for the first volume of Holinshed's *Chronicles* (1577).
Later, he traveled to the Continent where he lived almost the
remainder of his life.[93] In 1582 he published at Leyden *Thee
First Foure Bookes of Virgil His Aeneis Translated Into English Heroical Verse, wythe oother Poetical diuises theretoo annexed.*[94] This impossible translation of the *Aeneid,* which is
neither English nor Irish but only Stanihurst, was justly parodied
by Thomas Nash in his introduction to Robert Greene's *Mena-
phon* (1589):

Then did he make, heauen's vault to rebounde, with rounce robble
    hobble
Of ruffe raffe roaring, with thwick thwack thurlery bouncing.[95]

The "oother Poetical diuises theretoo annexed" are Conceits,
Epitaphs, a sonnet by Lord Offaly, psalm-versification, and
translations of a number of the Latin epigrams of Sir Thomas
Moore. A fair sample is "Syr Thomas Moore His receipt for a
strong breath translated owt of his Latin Epigrames":

> First for a strong sauoure stincking, a *leeke* may be taken:
> That sent too bannish, thee best is an *Onion* eaten.
> And toe repeal lykwise that sauoure, garlik is holsoom.
> If that theese simples wyl not thee filthod abandon,
> A *rose,* or els nothing that drafty infirmitye cureth.[96]

The most interesting of the "Poetical diuises" is

An Epitaph Entityled *Commune Defunctorum,* such as oure vn-
learned *Rythmours* accustomablye make vpon thee death of every
Tom Tyler, as yf yt were a *last* for euerye one his *foote,* in which thee
quantities of syllables are not to be heeded;

[93] *DNB.*
[94] Republished by Edward Arber in *The English Scholar's Library of Old and
Modern Works,* #10.
[95] *Ibid.,* p. xviii.
[96] *Ibid.,* p. 145.

perhaps a parody on Anglo-Irish poetasters of the day. It is so-called, at any rate, by Crofton Croker and Seymour;[97] but it would seem to me to apply equally to English and Irish, Stani-hurst himself not excluded. He is plain in his own lines:

> Coom toe me, you *muses,* and thow most chieflye, *Minerua,*
> And ye that are dwellers in dens of darckned *Auerna:*
> Help mye pen in wryting, a death moste soarye reciting,
> Of the good old *Topas,* soon too thee mightye syr *Atlas.*[98]

and so on for twenty-five more lines. He is more amusing in his prose denunciation of petty rhymers:

> . . . are there not [he asks] diuerse skauingers of draftye poetrye in this oure age, that bast theyre papers with smearie larde sauoring al too geather of thee frynig pan? . . . Good God what a frye of such *wooden rythmours* dooth swarme in stacioners shops, who neauer enstructed in any grammar schoole, not atayning too thee paringes of thee Latin or Greeke tongue, yeet lyke blynd bayards rush on forward, fostring theyre vayne conceites wyth such ouerweening silly follyes, as they reck not too bee condemned of thee learned for igno-rant, so they bee commended of thee ignorant for learned.[99]

Of more worth than any of Stanihurst's own poems is "A Penitent Sonnet Written by thee *Lord Girald* a little beefore his death," included among the "Poetical diuises." This Gerald, Baron of Offaly, died in 1580 at the age of twenty-one, and Stanihurst liked his poem well enough to publish it. In the first stanza the young nobleman laments the loss of character that gamblers suffer, and the oaths and blasphemies they give way to. In the second stanza he laments for himself as one of them:

> There is no wight that vsed yt more,
> Than *hee* that wrote this verse;
> Who cryeth, *peccaui,* now therefore
> His othes his hert doe perce.
> Therefor example take by *mee,*

---

[97] Croker, *op. cit.,* pp. 138–39; Seymour, *op. cit.,* p. 95.
[98] Arber, *op. cit.,* p. 154.
[99] *Ibid.,* pp. 9–10.

That curse thee luckless tyme;
That eauer *dice* myn eyes dyd see,
Which bred in mee this *crime*.
Pardon mee for that is past,
I wyl offend no more:
In this moste vile and sinful *cast,*
Which I wyl stil abhore.[100]

Nothing else is in Stanihurst to delay us here. His contributions
to Holinshed [101] are considered below; [102] they are of value historically, but show him prejudiced against Ireland. His sym-
pathies lay mostly with England; and although, contrary to the
general practice of the day, he sometimes tries to interpret Ireland from the Irish point of view, he never quite succeeds.

We should like to be able to include John Derricke (*fl.* 1578)
and James Shirley (1596–1666) as Irish poets along with Stanihurst. Both these men, however, were Englishmen whose poetry
about Ireland was written simply because of the accident of
their being in Ireland for a few years and they cannot in strict-
ness be called Irish poets. Shirley, moreover, is a dramatist and
as such outside the scope of this study. But since Derricke's
The Image of Ireland, with a Discovery of the Woodkern
(1581) has been classed by Sir Samuel Ferguson as Irish literature [103] and Shirley's *St. Patrick for Ireland* (1639) makes use
of recognized Irish material, some slight discussion of their work
is not altogether out of place.

Derricke, said to have been a protégé of Sir Philip Sidney, to
whom he dedicated *The Image,* designed his poem as a satirical
picture of the Ulster woodkern. The first part pictures Ireland

[100] Arber, p. 154.

[101] "A Treatise containing a Plaine and Perfect Description of Ireland," pp.
1–69, and "A Continuation of the Chronicles of Ireland from the end of
Giraldus Cambrensis comprising the Reigne of King Henrie the Eightth,"
pp. 273–320: both in Vol. VI of Holinshed's *Chronicles,* London, 1808.

[102] See p. 62.

[103] Sir Samuel Ferguson, "Curiosities of Irish Literature: The Mere Irish,"
Dublin University Magazine, IX (1837), 546–58.

as inhabited with fawns and nymphs, into whose midst Jove decrees shall come the woodkern. It progresses with a discussion of the horses, cattle, and natural resources of the land, and closes with a eulogy to Sir Philip Sidney. The second part describes a battle between the English and the Irish, greatly to the disadvantage of the latter. The spirit of the work is shown by St. Patrick's being asked why he wasted time killing the snakes of Ireland,

> When as thou left'st more spitefull beasts [men]
> Within this fertile land.[104]

James Shirley, because London was plague-ridden, spent the years from 1636 to 1640 in Dublin. His residence there was opportune, for his friend Ogilby, Wentworth's Master of the Revels, had opened in 1635 the new theater in Werburgh Street, the first in Dublin. Shirley wrote four pieces for the Dublin stage: "The Royal Master," "Rosania, or Love's Victory" (published as "The Doubtful Heir"), "The Constant Maid," and "St. Patrick for Ireland." [105]

The story of "St. Patrick for Ireland," the only play of Shirley's in which we are interested, is about Patrick's landing in Ireland, his overcoming of the power of the hostile druids, and his subsequent conversion of the island. In the first and best act the growing fears of Archimagus, the high priest, and his two attendant magicians are displayed at the news of Patrick's approach. Archimagus has a prophecy of old that foretells the coming of the Saint:

> A man shall come into this land
> With shaven crown, and in his hand
> A crooked staff; he shall command
> And in the east his table stand:
> From his warm lips a stream shall flow,

---

[104] *Ibid.,* p. 548.

[105] F. G. Fleay, *A Biographical Chronicle of the English Drama 1559–1642,* pp. 242–45; A. H. Nason, *James Shirley, Dramatist,* pp. 91 ff.

To make rocks melt, and churches grow,
Where, while he sings, our gods shall bow,
And all our kings his law allow.

The High King of Ireland, Leogarius, has a dream in which he sees

> . . . a pale man coming from the sea
> Attended by a tribe of reverend men.

In his dream, all save the High King do homage to the stranger. Archimagus, when he hears the dream, tells the King that the demons of his priests will shortly do away with Patrick, but when the Saint enters the King's court the demons are powerless. Still Archimagus is not dismayed, and the act ends with his renewed promises that Patrick will be overcome and that the King has nothing to fear from him. Through the remaining four acts Patrick moves in a maze of magic, tricks, and burnings, but emerges triumphant. The play is one of Shirley's poorer ones, and, as I have said above, has pertinence for us only in that it uses Irish material for its subject. Shirley's source was probably Jocelin's life of Patrick, published at Paris in 1624.[106]

[106] "A Latin Narrative of the Life and Miracles of St. Patrick," printed by Thomas Massingham in *Florilegum Insulae Sanctorum,* Paris, 1624. See also Hugh Macmullan, "The Sources of Shirley's *St. Patrick for Ireland," PMLA,* September 1933, pp. 808–14.

The Seventeenth Century: Fingal, Forth, and Bargy

SEVERAL seventeenth-century poems done in the dialect spoken in Fingal and in the baronies of Forth and Bargy have come down to us. The name "Fingal," meaning "the land of the Norseman, or foreigner," was used for the English Pale generally; it referred actually to the coastal land some miles north of Dublin. Fynes Moryson speaks of it thus: "And to the North [from Dublin] lies Fengall, a little Territory, as it were the garner of the Kingdome, which is environed by the Sea and great Rivers, and this situation hath defended it from the incursion of Rebels in former civill warres." [107] Arthur Young, writing in 1778, defines Fingal as "a territory near Dublin, extending along the coast, inhabited by a people they call Fingallians; an English colony planted here many years ago, speaking nearly the same language as the Barony of Forth, but more intermixed with Irish in language, etc., from vicinity to the capital." [108]

Both Fingal and the baronies of Forth and Bargy in south county Wexford evidently gave way only in part to the Irish language and customs; hence, the inhabitants of these districts kept largely their own speech. Stanihurst is detailed about it:

To this day [*ca.* 1577] the dregs of the old ancient Chaucer English are kept as well there [Forth and Bargy] as in Fingal, as they term a spider, an attercop; a wisp, a wad; a lump of bread, a pocket or picket; a sillibuck, a coprous; a faggot, a blease, or a blaze; . . . a physician, a leach; a gap, a shard; a base court or quadrangle, a bawen, or . . . a barton. . . .[109]

---

[107] *Op. cit.,* IV, 188–89.
[108] Quoted by Hogan, *op. cit.,* p. 39.
[109] Holinshed's *Chronicles,* London, 1808, VI, 4.

That Forth and Bargy spoke their old dialect down through the eighteenth century appears in the following excerpt from a letter written by an Englishman traveling in Ireland about the middle of that century:

These ancient English that are planted here [Wexford], have something peculiar to themselves. The English they speak seems to be that of Geofrey Chaucer, Robert of Gloster, or the Monk of Lithgate, as it is hard to be understood. The Inhabitants of Wexford indeed have it not so much; but I speak of those we meet with in the Country, and those we see at Market.[110]

Curtis has it that the dialect lasted well into the nineteenth century, claiming that the inhabitants of Forth and Bargy "spoke their distinctive Chaucerian and earlier English speech to 1860"; he describes the dialect as "simply an early form of English derived from the western and south-western counties of England, from which Dublin, the towns, and large parts of the colony were generally populated." [111] Heuser believes this speech to be a direct descendant of the language used in the Kildare poems.[112]

The extant poems done in the Fingallian and the Forth and Bargy dialect are headed by James Farewell's *The Irish Hudibras, or Fingallian Prince, Taken from the Sixth Book of Virgil's Aeneids, and Adapted to the Present Times,* printed at London in 1689. Jeremiah Hogan, in his discussion of Fingallian, says that this poem seems to be the only surviving record of that dialect.[113] But Hogan has overlooked other poems that have the word "Fingallian" in their titles and may therefore be examples of the dialect. Crofton Croker mentions a seventeenth-century piece in manuscript Sloan 900 called "The Fingallian Hunting of the Hare"; [114] and in the same manuscript, ap-

[110] W. R. Chetwood, ed., *A Tour through Ireland* . . . by Two English Gentlemen, 2nd ed., pp. 168–69.

[111] *Studies,* VIII, 247–48.

[112] *Die Kildare-Gedichte,* pp. 56 ff.

[113] *Op. cit.,* p. 39.

[114] *Op. cit.,* p. 208.

parently not noticed by Croker, are two other seventeenth-century poems, "The Fingallian Dance" [115] and "The Fingallian Travesty, or the Sixth Book of Virgill's Aeneids, a la mode de Fingaule." [116] I have not seen the Sloan manuscript; it is probable that "The Fingallian Travesty" is the same poem as the printed *Irish Hudibras,* although from the unlikeness in the wording of the titles the manuscript copy may have in it a number of variant readings. We have, however, from Croker a one-stanza specimen of "The Fingallian Hunting of the Hare" (the dying hare is the speaker):

> But in a fine mead, she being almost spent,
> She made her last will, ay, and testament.
> "Cropt cur, with thee," says she, "I will not stay:
> Nor with true running Cutty, that showed such fair play;
> But to thee, brave Hector, I yield up my life."
> And so Hector bore her, and ended the strife.[117]

The only dialectal peculiarity observable in these lines is the possible accent on the "-ment" of "testament," and that involves a far-fetched scansion. But without the entire poem, we cannot say definitely that it lacks the characteristics of *The Irish Hudibras.*

In his preface to this last-named poem, Farewell gives his definition of Fingal and we find that he means by it simply the Pale:

Fingaul, i.e. Finis Galliae, viz. the Confines, Bounds and Limits of the Gauls in Ireland: It extends from the County of Dublin, and part of Westmeath [Meath?], by the Seacoast; and is called the English Pale, the Ancient Habitation of the Gauls. [They are] the old Eng-

[115] Samuel Ayscough, *A Catalogue of the Manuscripts . . . in the British Museum,* II, 836.

[116] *Ibid.,* II, 828. It is odd that Croker did not mention "The Fingallian Dance," for it and "The Fingallian Hunting of the Hare" are catalogued together.

[117] *Op. cit.,* p. 208.

lish, called Gauls, now Fingallians, to distinguish them from the Native Irish. . . .[118]

Further on he gives not only his reasons for choosing Fingal as the scene of his poem, but also his qualifications for his job:

This harmless Spot (not Ireland) is Chosen for the Scene of the Comedy, to avoid a National Reflection. Nor will an ingenious Disposition find any occasion of Affront; it being not only Encourag'd, but carry'd on by the best sort of Gentlemen-Natives of the place, when the foundations of this Shallow-work was first laid; at whose Houses this Author was often entertain'd, to find out their Language, Sports, and Customs.[119]

The poem is a coarse satire on the Irish. Nees, the hero, on his trip through hell, which he enters by way of St. Patrick's Purgatory in Lough Derg, finds many prominent Irishmen and heroes of Irish mythology in places supposedly appropriate. For instance,

> And there was Osker, great Mac Osin
> Who was to great O Fin near Cousin:
> His Fathers—Brothers—Uncles Bard,
> Call'd for that cause, his own Bas-tard.[120]
>
> . . .
>
> And here was that prodigious Tooll,
> That monstrous Geant, Finn Mac-Heuyle,
> Whose Carcass bury'd in the Meadows,
> Took up nine Acres of Pottados.[121]

So far as the poetry of the poem goes, these lines are a fair sample. But only one dialectal peculiarity is shown: the accent on the second syllable of "Bas-tard." Some lines appearing earlier in the poem are more representative of the dialecticisms used rather plentifully throughout:

> One Courtesie I must demand,
> Since Here's de Passage to dat Land;

[118] *The Irish Hudibras,* p. ii.
[119] *Ibid.,* p. iii.
[120] *Ibid.,* p. 85.
[121] *Ibid.,* p. 86.

And here is Nees beg dy Par-doon,
Dat I choos dee for my Gar-soon;
Dat I may pass de black Va-teer,
Once more to see my old Fa-deer; . . .[122]

In this selection the peculiarities fall into three groups: *d* for *th*, *v* for *w*, and accentuation on the last syllable of two-syllable words that in standard English are accented on the first syllable. Examination of the remainder of the poem shows *t* for *th*, *s* for *sh*, etc. These five groups seem to be those into which the dialecticisms most frequently fall.

But a dialect showing these characteristics does not seem to have been unique to Fingal. The celebrated "Lillibullero" that mocked the Irish Catholics and was sung by all of England during the revolution of 1688 exhibits striking similarities of language to *The Irish Hudibras*. The opening lines go as follows:

Ho, broder Teague, dost hear de decree,
    Lillibullero, bullena a-la,
Dat we shall have a new Deputee,
    Lillibullero, bullena a-la . . .
Ho, by Shaint Tyburne, it is de Talbote,
    Lillibullero, etc.
And he will cut de Englishman's troate.
    Lillibullero, etc.
Dough by my sowl de English do prat
    Lillibullero, etc.
De law's on dare side, and Christ knows what;
    Lillibullero, etc.
But if de dispense do come from de Pope.
    Lillibullero, etc.
We'll hang *Magna Charta,* and them in a rope.
    Lillibullero, etc.[123]

Likewise, examination of contemporary English plays, such as Jonson's *The Irish Masque* (1613), Howard's *The Committee*

[122] *Ibid.,* p. 20.
[123] Sir Charles Gavan Duffy, *The Ballad Poetry of Ireland,* 3rd ed., Introduction, p. xvi.

(1665), and Farquhar's *Twin Rivals* (1703), shows that the Irish dialect used by characters on the English stage bore the same characteristics.[124] Moreover, Croker, quoting Windle, speaks of a patois used in Cork.

The vernacular of this region [Cork] may be regarded as the ancient cockneyism of the mixed race who held the old city—Danes, English, and Irish. It is a jargon, whose principal characteristic appears in the pronunciation of *th*, as exemplified in *dis, dat, den, de.*[125]

In addition, we know nothing of James Farewell. To judge from the lines of his preface quoted above, he was at best only a visitor to the homes of the gentry in Fingal. Nor should it be forgotten that the specimen of "The Fingallian Hunting of the Hare" has but one, and that a doubtful one, of the language characteristics of *The Irish Hudibras*. And finally, the testimony of Stanihurst and Young,[126] both of whom based their statements on firsthand knowledge, that the dialect of Fingal was similar to that of Forth and Bargy must be given primary importance, for the song given below in the Forth and Bargy dialect bears little similarity in language to *The Irish Hudibras*.

All this evidence points to a three-fold conclusion: 1) that *The Irish Hudibras* is not written in the Fingallian dialect, but in the dialect characteristic generally of the Anglo-Irish in the seventeenth century; 2) that the extant poems in the Forth and Bargy dialect should be regarded as representative also of the dialect spoken in Fingal; 3) that no example of this Fingal, Forth, and Bargy dialect, written in Fingal, has survived.

The extant poems in the Forth and Bargy dialect are definitely distinctive in language.[127] What we know of that dialect begins with the work of Charles Vallancey,[128] who published in 1788

---

[124] See W. J. Lawrence, "Irish Types in Old-time English Drama," *Anglia,* XXXV (1912), 347-56.

[125] *Op. cit.,* p. 169.

[126] See above, p. 37.

[127] See Heuser's discussion, *Die Kildare-Gedichte,* pp. 56-60.

[128] "Memoir of the Language, Manners and Customs of an Anglo-Saxon Colony settled in the Baronies of Forth and Bargie, in the county of Wexford,

an essay on the inhabitants of Forth and Bargy that included a list of about four hundred dialectal words and "An Old Song" in the dialect. "An Old Song," together with a few other poems of the same kind collected by Jacob Poole about 1800, was edited and published by William Barnes in 1867.[129] Two stanzas of "An Old Song," followed by a translation, will show the quality of the dialect:

> Well, gosp, c'hull be zeid; mot thee fartoo, and fade;
> He deight ouse var gabble, tell ee zin go t'glade.
> Ch'am a stouk, an a donel; wou'll leigh out ee dey,
> Th 'valler w'speen here, th 'lass ee chourch-hey.
> . . .
> Mot w'all 'ar boust, hi soon was ee teight
> At 'ar errone was var ameing 'ar 'ngish I height
> Zitch vezzen, tarvizzen 'till than w' ne'er zey
> Nore zichel, n'eer well nowe nore n'eer mey.
>
> (Well, gossip, it shall be told; you ask what ails me,
>   and for what;
> You have out us in talk, till the sun goes to set.
> I am a fool and a dunce; we'll idle out the day.
> The more we spend here, the less in the churchyard.
>
> But with all their bravado they were soon taught
> That their errand was aiming to bring anguish upon 'em.
> Such driving and struggling till then we ne'er saw,
> Nor such never will, no, nor never may.) [130]

Nothing very much like *The Irish Hudibras* is observable in this excerpt; obviously the Forth and Bargy dialect, with which we have now associated the Fingallian dialect, was a unique

---

Ireland, in 1167, 1168 and 1169," *Transactions of the Royal Irish Academy,* 1788, II, section "Antiquities," 19–41.

[129] *A Glossary;* With some pieces of verse of the Old Dialect of the English Colony in the baronies of Forth and Bargy, county of Wexford, Ireland. Formerly collected by Jacob Poole, edited now by William Barnes.

[130] Vallancey, *op. cit.,* pp. 36–37.

speech. Their uniqueness, however, is as much as we can say for these lines; they have no poetic merit.

For final consideration in the seventeenth century, the historical songs written about the revolution of 1688, collected and published by Croker,[131] remain. Of the songs Croker prints, only two can be said reliably to be of Irish authorship. They are "King James's Welcome to Ireland" and "The Boyne Water." These have a rude vigor and swing that bespeak their popular origin. Both are better than average; the opening stanza of "King James's Welcome" is by no means bad verse:

> Play, piper—play, piper,
>   Come, lasses, dance and sing,
> And old harpers strike up
>   To harp for the king.
> He is come—he is come,
>   Let us make Ireland ring
> With a loud shout of welcome,
>   May God save the king.[132]

And "The Boyne Water" was known and liked by Sir Walter Scott, who could make when the occasion demanded a "vigorous recitation" [133] of its ten stanzas, of which the first is a good sample:

> July the first, in Oldbridge Town,
>   There was a grievous battle,
> Where many a man lay on the ground,
>   By the cannons that did rattle.
> King James he pitched his tent between
>   The lines for to retire;
> But King William threw his bomb-balls in
>   And set them all on fire.[134]

*   *   *   *   *   *   *   *   *   *

131 "The Historical Songs of Ireland," *Percy Society Publications*, Vol. I.
132 *Ibid.*, p. 29.
133 *Ibid.*, p. 59.
134 *Ibid.*, p. 60. And see W. B. Yeats, "Lapis Lazuli," *Collected Poems*, New York, 1956, p. 292, line 7.

So much for our discussion of Irish poetry from the English invasion to 1700. Its small volume is, as has been pointed out above, largely explained by the struggle between the English and Gaelic languages. Three other reasons help, however, in the explanation: 1) the destruction of manuscripts that must have taken place in the almost constant wars and troubles; 2) the disappearance or destruction of manuscripts at the time of the dissolution of the monasteries; 3) the late coming to Ireland of the art of printing-from-movable-type. The first press was set up in Dublin in 1550 by Humphrey Powell.[135]

Some additional information can be gleaned from Stanihurst's, Harris's, and Dix's lists of Irish writers and books. Stanihurst, in his "Description of Ireland," names five poets writing in English of whom he knew or of whom he had heard:

Dormer, a lawyer, borne in Rosse, scholar of Oxford, he writ in ballat roiall, "The decaie of Rosse."

Macgrane, a schoolmaster in Dublin, he wrote carols and sundrie ballads.

William Nugent . . . wrote in the English toong diverse sonnets.

There liveth one Wise in Waterford, that maketh verie well in the English. Andrew Wise a toward youth, and a good versefier.

Sutton, one of that name, is a verie good maker in English.[136]

Although I have been unable to locate the poetry of any of these five, I think our definition of Irish poetry—poetry in the English language written by an Irishman or Anglo-Irishman and inspired by Ireland or its people—would include their work. For Stanihurst, writing about 1577, would be talking of the "old" English; i.e., those English who had been in Ireland for a generation or more and had come to regard it as their home. These old English must be sharply differentiated from the un-

---

[135] See E. R. M'Clintock Dix, "Humfrey Powell, the First Dublin Printer," *Proceedings of the Royal Irish Academy,* XXVII (August 1908), section C, 7, pp. 213–16.

[136] Holinshed's *Chronicles,* London, 1808, VI, 59–66.

dertakers and adventurers of the next century who never for-
got they were Englishmen and whose descendants in many
cases continued to regard England as their home and Ireland
as a stopover.

Stanihurst's list was added to considerably by Sir James Ware
in his *De Scriptoribus Hibernia* (1639) that Walter Harris,
Ware's grandson-in-law, revised and brought down to the year
1700. But Ware's and Harris's list must be treated with caution.
The full title of Ware's volume as translated by Harris is "The
History of the Writers of Ireland, In two books, viz.: I. Such
Writers who were born in that Kingdom. And, II. Such who,
though Foreigners, enjoyed Preferments or Offices there, or had
their Education in it. . . ." The list includes names like Sir
John Denham, Nahum Tate, and George Farquhar, all of
whom, from our point of view, are English writers. Sticking
to our definition we rule out all but two:

Edmund Dwyer, titular Bishop of Limerick, writ two small pieces of
Poetry in Hexameter and Pentameter Measure, one, on the miracles
of St. Brigid, and the other, on the inextinguishable Fire of St. Brigid
at Kildare.

There was another Person of the same Name and Surname [Luke
Wadding], who was born (I think) in the County of Wexford, was
titular Bishop of Ferns, Doctor of Sorbonne, a Secular Priest, and
buried in the Franciscan Convent at Wexford. He published in the
reign of King Charles II. *A small Garland of pious and godly Songs
for the Solace of his Friends and Neighbours in their Afflictions.*[137]

Finally, from E. R. M'Clintock Dix's *Catalogue of Early
Dublin-Printed Books, 1601–1700,*[138] a few more titles and

---

[137] Sir James Ware, *The History of the Writers of Ireland. Written in Latin
. . . translated by Walter Harris,* Dublin, 1764, pp. 95–140.
[138] The *Catalogue* was published in four parts and a supplement: Part I,
Dublin, 1898; Part II, Dublin, 1899; Part III, Dublin, 1902; Part IV, Dublin,
1905; Supplement, Dublin, 1912. A two-page appendix to Part I was printed
at the end of Part II. In the copy used here, Parts I–III were bound as Volume I;
Part IV and the Supplement as Volume II. The page numbering is continuous.

names can be added. Nothing further about any of these entries was available.

1624   Revd Stephen Jerome, Domestick Chappleine to the Rt. Hon. Earle of Corke. Ireland's Jubilee, or Io-Paean, for Prince Charles, his welcome home, etc. The Societie of Stationers, printer.

1625   Alexander Spicer. An Elegy on the Much Lamented Death of The Right Hon. Sir Arthur Chichester Knight, etc. The Soc. of Stationers, printer.

1626   Anon. Mount Taragh's Triumph. To the Tune of the Careere. A Ballad with a woodcut of a Harp.

1630   Musarum Lachrymae. Poems in Hebrew, Greek, Latin, and English by twenty-four students of Trinity College, Dublin. The Societie of Stationers, printer.

1649   Ormonde's Breakfast, or a true relation of the Salley and Skirmish performed by Collonell Michl. Jones and his Party, against the Marquess of Ormonde and his Forces encamped before Dublin, the 2nd of August, 1649. In a Dialogue between a Chevalier and a Roundhead. In rhyme.

1661   F.S. (Francis Synge or Singe) A Panegyrick on the Most Auspicious . . . Return of . . . James Duke, Marquess and Earl of Ormond & c. . . . John Crook, printer.

1661   Jo. Jones, B.A., T.C.D. Elegies 1 English 3 Latin on the . . . Death of the . . . Earl of Mountrath (Chas. Coote). John Crook, printer.

1663   Poems by Several Persons of Quality and refined wits.

1667   Revd. Lemuel Mathews. A Pandarique Elegie Upon the death of . . . Jeremye Late Lord Bishop of Doune Connor and Dromore. John Crook, printer.

1669   Lt. Col. Wm. Mercer. A Welcome in a Poem to . . . John Lord Roberts, Baron of Truro, Ld. Lieutenant General & General Governor of Ireland & c. Josiah Windsor, printer.[139]

1670   Thomas Flatman. On the Death of the True, Valiant, and Loyal George Duke of Albemarle . . . A Pindarique Ode. Benjamin Tooke, printer.[140]

---

[139] Dix, *Catalogue,* I, 23–138.
[140] *Ibid.,* II, 361.

1671 An Elegy and Funeral Oration on the death of the Revd. R. Lingard, Dean of Lismore & Public Professor of Divinity.

1674 Stanley Starkey (or Starkie). Upon the death of the Hon. & c. Sir Edward Massie & c. An Elegy in verse.[141]

1682 J(ohn) Wilson. To His Excellency Richard Earle of Arran & c. Lord Deputy of Ireland.

1685 An Elegy on the Death of the Right Honble. Richard *Butler,* Earl of Arran.

1685 To his Grace The Duke of Ormond, upon His leaving the Government and Kingdom of *Ireland.* Andrew Crook and Samuel Helsham, printer.

1686 Poem, upon the arrival of His Excellency, Henry Earl of Clarendon. . . . Andrew Crook and Samuel Helsham, printer.

1691 Ode to the King . . . Presented to the King upon His departure from Ireland. Jo. Brent, printer.

1691 J(ohn) S(tearne). Seasonable Thoughts in Passion Week. In Verse. Joseph Ray, printer.

1693 B.H., A.B., T.C.D. An Ode on the Anniversary of the Coronation of King Wm. & Queen Mary. Joseph Ray, printer.

1695 Stepney. A Poem Dedicated to . . . Her late . . . Majesty Queen Mary. Reprinted for Pk. Campbell.

1698 Charles Hopkins. Whitehall; or the Court of England; A Poem. Andrew Crook, printer.

1699 George Wilkins, A.B., T.C.D. The Chase of the Stagg. A Descriptionary Poem. Dedicated to the Duchess of Ormond. Josias Shaw, printer.

1699 Rev. Jas. Aickin, Master of a Private School near Essex Bridge. Londerias or a Narrative of the Siege of Londonderry, & c., & c. Written in Verse.[142]

And a last item from the catalogue of the Bradshaw collection of Irish books at Cambridge (this item is not given by Dix):

c.1691 Walsh (R.), To his Excellency Lieutenant General Ginckel Commander in Chief of all Their Majesties Forces in Ireland; upon His coming to Dublin.[143]

[141] *Ibid.,* I, 143–54.
[142] *Ibid.,* II, 193–380.
[143] *A Catalogue of the Bradshaw Collection of Irish Books in the University Library, Cambridge,* II, p. 696, #4110.

❧ 6 ❧

From 1700 to 1798

ALONG with the swift increase in the number of English-speaking Irish during the eighteenth century came a corresponding increase in the number of poets writing in English. Unfortunately, the improvement was only in numbers; with exceptions like Charlotte Brooke's *Reliques of Irish Poetry* in 1789, treated in Part II,[144] and the ballad and national poetry of '98,[145] the Irish poetry of the eighteenth century has perhaps even less distinction than the poetry from the invasion to 1700. Although a great many of the poets can be called Irish poets, since their work directly concerned Ireland or its people, they were for the most part utterly unoriginal in form or diction, aping slavishly the English poets.

An examination of Croker's *Popular Songs of Ireland*, that is devoted chiefly to eighteenth-century verse, furnishes proof of this statement. A few examples will help. Croker reprints as one of the best-known poems of its time "Molly Asthore," by George Ogle (1742–1814),[146] three lines of which are a fair sample:

As down by Banna's banks I strayed, one evening in May,
The little birds with blythest notes made vocal every spray;
They sung their little notes of love, they sung them o'er and
o'er. . . .[147]

And here is a stanza of a poem called "A new Ballad on the Hot Wells at Mallow," printed originally in *The Ulster Miscellany* (1753):

[144] See below, pp. 111–121.
[145] See Rolleston and Brooke, *A Treasury of Irish Poetry*, New York, 1905, p. x.
[146] D. J. O'Donoghue, *The Poets of Ireland*, p. 353.
[147] *Popular Songs of Ireland*, p. 135.

All you that are
Both lean and bare,
With scarce an ounce of tallow,
To make your flesh
Look plump and fresh,
Come drink the springs at Mallow.[148]

And here a few lines from "The Glass of Whiskey," that appeared in *The Sentimental and Masonic Magazine* for December 1793:

At the side of the road, near the bridge of Drumcondra,
Was Murrough O'Monaghan stationed to beg;
He brought from the wars, as his share of the plunder,
A crack on the crown, and the loss of a leg.[149]

A higher place, however, must be accorded to one of the poems in Croker's book, Thomas Mozeen's "The Kilruddery Hunt," that Ritson had thought good enough to include in his *Select Collection of English Songs* (1783),[150] calling it "The Irish Hunt." Ritson spoke of it as "the most exceptional" [151] Irish poem he knew. Mozeen published the poem originally in *A Collection of Miscellaneous Essays* (1762), under the title of "A Description of a Fox-Chase, that happened in the County of Dublin, 1744, with the Earl of Meath's Hounds. A Ballad. Tune, *Shelah Nagirah*." [152] Mozeen, Irish actor and singer, wrote some other verse and a farce that he called "Antigallican"; [153] but his hunting poem is the only piece of any worth that he did. The vigor and swing of the lines fully justify Ritson's praise:

In seventeen hundred and forty and four,
The fifth of December—I think 'twas no more;

---

[148] *Popular Songs of Ireland*, p. 245.
[149] *Ibid.*, p. 81.
[150] II, 168–70.
[151] *Ibid.*, I, vii.
[152] Pp. 33–36.
[153] *A Collection of Miscellaneous Essays*, pp. 241–93.

At five in the morning, by most of the clocks,
We rode from Kilruddery to try for a fox . . .
Ten minutes past nine was the time o' the day,
When Reynard unkennelled, and this was his play . . .
Bray Common he passed, leaped Lord Anglesea's wall,
And seemed to say, "Little I value you all." [154]

The nine eight-line stanzas carry through to the kill and end
with the customary all-night drinking bout. Part of the piece
still retains some popularity.[155]

Consideration in some detail of two eighteenth-century Irish
poets, Laurence Whyte and Samuel Whyte (no relation), whose
work was popular enough to call for second editions, gives more
evidence of the way in which English styles and influences pre-
dominated. The first, Laurence Whyte (d. 1755), a native of
Westmeath and a schoolmaster,[156] published in 1740 *Original
Poems on Various Subjects, Serious and Diverting*.[157] The
principal poem in the book is an "Essay on Dunning," in five
cantos, and a quotation from it about the respective qualities of
blank verse and rhyme shows the literary influences that had
most effect on Whyte:

Thy Aid, O Butler! help me Swift!
Here give your Bard a gentle lift,
Wh'admires your Measure short and sweet,
Which moves along with nimble feet,
And travels further in good Rhyme,
Than stately Blank in twice the Time;
More comprehensive, and much stronger,
Than some whose strides are two foot longer . . .[158]

Later in the poem Whyte, who seems to have been alive to the
conditions of his native land, takes a fling at one of its worst

[154] Croker, *op. cit.*, p. 211.
[155] It is used, for instance, in McConathy, Meissner, etc., *The Music Hour*,
Third Book, New York, 1929, pp. 92–93.
[156] O'Donoghue, *op. cit.*, p. 480.
[157] Dublin.
[158] Whyte, *op. cit.*, 2nd ed., p. 8.

evils—absenteeism, almost seventy years before Maria Edge-
worth attacked the same evil in *The Absentee:*

> These Absentees we here describe
> Are mostly of our Ir-sh Tribe,
> Who live in Luxury and Pleasure,
> And throw away their Time and Treasure,
> Cause Poverty and Devastation,
> And sink the Credit of the Nation,
> . . . our Gentry all run wild,
> And never can be reconcil'd,
> To live at home upon their Rent,
> With any Pleasure or Content . . .[159]

Elsewhere he writes "A Divine Poem on the Nativity of our
Lord and Saviour Jesus Christ, written December the 25th,
1733," [160] done in heroic couplets and inspired, of course, by
Milton; [161] "Critical Annotations" [162] on various writers and
foods; and sundry other pieces.[163] A second edition of the poems
appeared in 1742.

The other Whyte, Samuel (1733–1811), was a Dublin peda-
gogue and litterateur who conducted for over fifty years a sem-
inary for young ladies and gentlemen at 75 Grafton Street.[164]
His influence and ability as a teacher were attested by his pupil,
Thomas Moore, who spoke of Whyte as "at the head of his profession in [Dublin] . . . [I owe] . . . to that exalted person
all the instruction in English literature I have ever received." [165]

---

[159] Whyte, *op. cit.,* 2nd ed., p. 97.

[160] *Ibid.,* pp. 193–95.

[161] Cf., *e.g.,* Whyte's line 48 "Whose great Redemption from your Birth
began" with Milton's "Our great redemption from above did bring" (l. 4 of the
"Nativity").

[162] Whyte, *op. cit.,* p. 153.

[163] In Croker's notes to "A Kerry Pastoral," *Percy Society Publications,* VII,
19, he speaks of Whyte's "faithful picture of the state of Irish society" in
Whyte's "The Parting Cup." Croker's judgment might be questioned in this
instance.

[164] *DNB.*

[165] Thomas Moore, *Memoirs of Richard Brinsley Sheridan,* I, 3.

Whyte's chief works were *The Shamrock: or, Hibernian Cresses,* a collection of poems published in Dublin in 1772, reprinted in London in a pirated edition in 1774,[166] and republished in Dublin, together with additional material, in 1792-94; [167] *The Theatre, a Didactic Essay,* published in 1790 and republished in the same volume with *The Shamrock* in 1792–94; and *Miscellanea Nova,* Dublin, 1801. The man's literary interests were wide, his publications range from pretty little saccharin lyrics to semi-scientific research into the sources of *Paradise Lost.* Yet nowhere does he show any real consciousness of Ireland or the Irish; Dublin and its environs seem to have been all he knew of that country, and he looked on Dublin as an English city.

The Shamrock was probably the book by which he was best known in his day; the poems in it that seem to be Whyte's are of very little worth but they are not quite so bad as one recent critic makes out.[168] Once in a while he could do lines like these: lines like these:

> 'Tis Night, dead Night; and o'er the Plain
> Darkness extends her ebon Ray,
> While wide along the gloomy Scene
> Deep Silence holds her solemn Sway.[169]

Curiously, two of Whyte's poems have been claimed as being "symptoms" in the "Celtic Revival" that occurred in English literature during the years from 1760 to 1800, but such claim is rather far-fetched.[170] Samuel was completely unaware of any-

---

[166] *A collection of poems, the production of the kingdom of Ireland; selected from a collection pub. in that kingdom, intituled, The Shamrock; or, Hibernian cresses.* The 2d ed. London, R. Snagg, 1774.

[167] *A Collection of Poems . . . with Notes.*

[168] Howard Mumford Jones, *The Harp That Once-,* p. 19.

[169] *The Shamrock,* p. 169.

[170] E. D. Snyder, *The Celtic Revival in English Literature 1760–1800,* p. 125. The two poems Snyder mentions are "Ode on British Freedom" (*The Shamrock,* pp. 207–16) and "The Hone: A Piece of Irish Mythology" (*The Shamrock,* pp. 340–42). The "Ode" is a history of the struggles by the inhabitants of the British Isles for freedom and in tracing that history mentions the Druids; "The Hone" is an extended pun on the word "ochone."

thing Celtic in the life of Ireland. His outlook and his life were
bound up with the English ascendancy; all the influences observable in his poetry were English; and his great god among
poets was Milton.[171]

The poems in *The Shamrock* that were not written by Whyte
are rather difficult to spot since he mentions no author but himself by name, and then only as the editor. Apparently one of
them is "Mully of Mountown," that Ritson reprinted in his
English Anthology [172] and attributed to William King. The
style is unique for *The Shamrock,* and the poem is the best in
the book. The opening lines are a pleasant picture:

> Mountown! thou sweet Retreat from Dublin Cares,
> Be famous long for Apples and for Pears;
> For Turnips, Carrots, Lettuce, Beans and Peas,
> For Peggy's Butter, and for Peggy's Cheese . . .
> May fat Geese gaggle round thy cramm'd Barn Door,
> Nor e'er want Apple Sauce, and Mustard Store;
> Ducks in thy Ponds, and Chickens in thy Penns;
> And be thy Turkies numerous as thy Hens.[173]

Examples of the kind of poetry the two Whytes wrote could
easily be multiplied, but to very little profit. These two are, as
a matter of fact, above the average. Below them in poetic ability
are Irish poets like Thomas Dermody (1755–1802) whose two
volumes, euphemistically called by their editor *The Harp of
Erin,*[174] it is possible to go through without stumbling on anything that even faintly resembles poetry.

The indefatigable Crofton Croker edited for the Percy Society several eighteenth-century Irish songs dealing with the
capture of Carrickfergus by Thurot in 1760,[175] and "A Pastoral

---

[171] See my article, "A Dublin Milton Enthusiast," *Modern Language Notes,*
April 1941, pp. 285–86.

[172] 3 vols., London, 1793–94, I, 144–48.

[173] *The Shamrock,* p. 5.

[174] 2 vols., London, 1804, edited by James Grant Richmond.

[175] *Percy Society Publications,* XXI, part II, "The Siege of Carrickfergus,"
pp. 10–13; "Thurot's Dream," pp. 17–19; and "The Capture of Carrickfergus,"
pp. 20–23.

in Imitation of the First Eclogue of Virgil" that had been originally published in Dublin in 1719.[176] Thurot, an Irish soldier
of fortune, in command of a French squadron of some half-
dozen vessels, captured Carrickfergus on February 21, 1760—
the first move in what the French hoped would be a successful
invasion of England. But a few days later, on February 26, an
English squadron engaged and defeated the French; in the battle Thurot was killed. The three songs Croker prints have only
historical interest to recommend them; this stanza from "The
Siege of Carrickfergus" is typical:

> The town then they took without any resistance,
>   The castle they thought was as easy likewise;
> So they came marching up in grand divisions,
>   To storm it, then guarded by the brave Irish boys.
> But we kept constant fire, and made them retire,
>   Till our ammunition entirely was gone;
> Then aloud we did say, brave boys let's away,
>   And sally out on them with sword in hand.[177]

"A Pastoral in Imitation of the First Eclogue of Virgil," in
praise of the provost, fellows, and scholars of Trinity College,
Dublin, is a gushy effusion of thanks for the college's part in
having the author's ancestral farm restored to him, and is worth
no more than mention.

Odds and ends of the oral literature of the century, better
than anything we have considered, are come upon sometimes
in Irish travel books of the day. Two such examples written down
about the middle of the century show the vitality such literature
generally has. The first was heard in Cork and concerns the
Duke of Grafton, son of Charles II, who was mortally wounded
in the siege and capture of that city by the Duke of Marlbor-
ough and who died October 9, 1690.

> Here fell Henry, Duke of Grafton
> As good a Blade as e'er had Haft on,

[176] Vol. VII, London, 1842.
[177] *Percy Society Publications*, XXI, part II, 11.

Or e'er made a Pass
At a lad or a Lass;
But a Bullet of Cork
Soon finished his Work.
Pox rot him
That shot him;
A Son of a Whore
That got him.
I'll say no more,
But here fell Henry, Duke of Grafton.[178]

The second was heard spoken in Kilkenny:

Fire, without Smoak,
Air, without Fog;
Water, without Mud,
And Land without Bog.[179]

*   *   *   *   *   *   *   *   *   *

The stream of mediocre Irish poetry throughout this century
can perhaps best be appreciated by a close reading of O'Donoghue's *Poets of Ireland*.[180] But the whole story of eighteenth-
century Irish poetry cannot be told without discussion of a new
influence that during these years was beginning to make itself
felt in Irish letters, an influence that was apart from and had no
effect on the kind of eighteenth-century poetry we have so far
considered. This influence, or force, first because of its own
power and then because of the subsidiary influence it stirred
into being, was ultimately to be responsible in large measure for
motivating the writers of the Celtic Revival of the nineteenth
century. But even during the eighteenth century it inspired some
Irish poetry of distinction, notably that of Charlotte Brooke.
We shall study her work in connection with an investigation of
the origins and growth of the new influence.

[178] W. R. Chetwood, ed., *op. cit.*, p. 62. Croker, "Historical Songs of Ireland,"
Percy Society Publications, I, 79, has a much longer and more anemic version.
[179] Chetwood, *op. cit.*, p. 183.
[180] On pp. 1–5, for example, he lists anonymous Irish poems and books of
poetry; of the sixty or more that belong to the eighteenth century, all have been
long forgotten—save by the curious.

Part II

THE MATTER OF IRELAND

Introduction

THAT new influence was the matter of Irish legend and literature, almost completely secreted in the Gaelic language from
the non-Gaelic-speaking Irish until the eighteenth and early
nineteenth centuries. Let us repeat what has been said above:
"The great mass of the natives . . . knew and recited the songs
of their own poets and retold in their own language the exploits
of Cuchulin and Finn, of Deirdre and Grania:—songs and
stories hidden from the English by the barrier of language." [1]
Not until these songs and stories were put into English did the
Anglo-Irish and the English-speaking Irish become familiar
with them. Too much emphasis cannot be placed on this point,
for it was the gradual widening and deepening of the stream
of that knowledge that brought about in large part the work
of W. B. Yeats and his fellow-writers at the turn of this century.

Very little attention has been paid to these men: the chroniclers, historians, and translators who put this native material
into English during the late sixteenth, the seventeenth, and
eighteenth centuries. They have been mentioned, if at all, chiefly
as curiosities; no attempt has been made to investigate and trace
the way in which their work brought a slow but steadily increasing knowledge of, and interest in, things Irish; nor has any
one pointed out how the line of descent runs from the earliest
chroniclers down to Standish James O'Grady and his *History of
Ireland* (1878–80), so often regarded as the spark that kindled
the flame of the modern literary revival in Ireland.[2] What

[1] P. 3.
[2] Ernest Boyd calls him "The Father of the Revival." See Boyd's *Ireland's
Literary Renaissance,* pp. 26–54. Yeats, *Autobiographies,* p. 272, speaks of him:
"In his unfinished *History of Ireland* he had made the old Irish heroes, Fion,
and Oisin, and Cuchullan, alive again. . . . Lady Gregory has told the same
tales . . . but O'Grady was the first, and we had read him in our 'teens."

Thomas Malory did for Arthurian legend, O'Grady did for Irish legend; and O'Grady, as Malory, had the precedence of the works of others on which to build his own work.

The comparison between the early English historians and the early Irish historians is an obvious one, for it was in the histories of Nennius, Geoffrey of Monmouth, William of Malmesbury, and others that the stories of Arthur and his knights were first made known; just as we shall find that it was in the histories of Campion, Hanmer, Keating, O'Halloran, and others that the stories of Deirdre, Cuchulin, and Finn were first made known. If the objection be raised that the English histories were in Latin and hence should properly be compared with the Irish histories in their original language—whether that language be Gaelic or English—whereas I am considering only English versions, the answer is twofold: first, the Gaelic language presented to the average Irishman unfamiliar with it a difficult barrier that he had very little desire to surmount, while the Latin language presented no difficulty to the educated Englishman of the Middle English period; second, the Irish writers of the nineteenth and twentieth centuries, the writers of the Celtic Revival, were men who in a majority of cases had but slight knowledge of Gaelic and would never have learned the old stories had they not been Englished.

In Part II, then, we shall trace the way in which the matter of Ireland was made available in English through the work of the historians, chroniclers, and translators from the third quarter of the sixteenth century to the end of the eighteenth. We shall discuss too the poetry of the period that was written in this tradition. When we speak of the English telling of Irish legends, we shall confine ourselves chiefly to the main tales of the Red Branch and the Finn cycles, for these are the stories that have meant most to the later Irish writers.

2

The Beginnings: Campion to Walsh

PROBABLY the first English telling of Irish legend appeared in Edmund Campion's *History of Ireland*. Campion (1540–81), who spent some months of his troubled life in Dublin, completed his history in the short space of ten weeks in 1571.[3] He gathered his material in the library of James Stanihurst, father of Richard, for in the preface he mentions the kindness and generosity of the older man.[4] Campion devotes but little space in his history to legends and tales for he regards them with contempt, yet what he does tell is of interest.

A race of giants, we learn, of the stock of Nimrod, came to Ireland about the same time as Bartolenus, one of Noah's progeny and a traditional early settler in Ireland. These giants, Campion says, set up their own government, kept the people in bondage, and were continually quarrelling with the rightful rulers of the land. Finally the rulers banded together against them, and in the succeeding great battle all the giants, save one, were destroyed. This one, Ruanus, was preserved,

who from time to time kept true record of their [the people of Ireland's] histories, else utterly done away by sundry casualties of death, warre, spoyle, fire, forraine victories, and he (forsooth) continued till the year of Christ 430. and told S. *Patrick* all the newes of the country requiring of him to bee baptized, and so died, when he had lived no more but two thousand and forty one yeares: which is twice the age of Methusalem.

So far Campion's form of the legend, but I cannot forbear quoting him further. "Had it been my chance in Ireland," he goes on with amusing satire, "to meete and confer with this noble Antiquarie, hee might have eased me of much travell." But

---

[3] *DNB.*

[4] Ware, ed., *Ancient Irish Histories,* Dublin, 1809, Vol. I, part 2.

legends should be looked at askance. "These things I note for
no other purpose but that the simple stumbling upon such
blinde legends should be warned to esteeme them as they are,
idle fantasies, wherewith some of their Poets, dallyed at the first,
and after through error and rudeness it was taken up for a sad
matter." [5]

We have here, obviously, part of the skeleton of the Finn cycle;
the gigantic statures of the heroes, for instance, is common
to all the stories of the Fenians. And Ruanus is of course Caoilte
MacRonain, in Keating's version of the story,[6] or Caeilte son of
Crunnchu in the version in *Silva Gadelica*.[7] Caoilte, along with
Oisin, survived the Fenians and lived on into the time of Patrick
with whom the two have the famous "Colloquy." [8]

Campion's history was slightly revised by Richard Stanihurst
and was published with Stanihurst's "Description of Ireland"
in Holinshed's *Chronicles* (1577).[9] Stanihurst makes no change
in the Ruanus story Campion told,[10] and that Stanihurst himself was familiar with some of the Finn stories we learn from
the following passage in the "Description":

There is in Meeth an hill called the hill of Taragh, Wherein is a plaine
twelve score long, which was named the Kempe his hall: there the
countrie had their meetings and folksmotes, as a place that was accounted the high palace of the monarch. The Irish historians hammer
manie fables in this forge of Fin Mac Coile and his Champions, as the
French historie dooth of king Arthur and the knights of the round
table.[11]

We would give a good deal had Stanihurst further identified the
Irish historians and told some of their fables.

[5] Ware, ed., *Ancient Irish Histories*, Dublin, 1809, Vol. I, part 2, pp. 33–34.

[6] *A General History of Ireland*, translated by Dermod O'Connor, p. 21.

[7] Ed. Standish Hayes O'Grady, London, 1892, II, 103.

[8] See "The Colloquy with the Ancients," *Silva Gadelica*, II, 101–265.

[9] See Stanihurst's dedication to his "Description" in Vol. VI of the *Chronicles*,
London, 1808.

[10] *Ibid.*, pp. 74–75.

[11] *Ibid.*, p. 39.

The anonymous sixteenth-century *Book of Howth*,[12] probably composed about the same time as Campion's history, speaks also of the Finn cycle but in much greater detail. As a matter of fact, the opening paragraph of the book gives the genealogy of Finn and Oisin. Here it is:

The genealogy of Fin Herin came out of Denmark, and landed at Falis-ni-Grye Barrerove, whose names are as followeth; viz., Davith the King, ancestor and father to Devre Done; and he had four sons, Covrrye, Boyskene, Fiaghe, and Oghe. And Boyskene had a son named Garreneslo; and the same Garre had a son named Con Caghmore; and the same Con had a son named Ferraloghe; and the same Ferraloghe had a son named Trenmore; and the same Trenmore had a son named Culle Negae; and the same Culle had a son named Fin Fa, otherwise called Fin Mac Culle, who had a son named Oshen, which told the same history to Saint Patrick. All these above-written of Fin Herin, except Davith, was born in Ireland. This Osseyne was alive in the year of our Lord 432.[13]

Further, it is told that the "soldiers called Fyen-erryne" were "appointed to keep the sea coasts . . . whose names . . . was Fin McKoyll, Kokoyllon, Keylte, Osker, McOsseyn, Dermot O'Dyne, Collemagh Morne, and divers others." [14] These are the chief names of the Fianna, dressed in queer spelling. They are easily recognizable as Finn MacCumhal, Caoilte, Osgar, Oisin, Diarmuid, and Goll MacMorna: the spelling "Kokoyllon" may be for Cuchulin, the placing of whose name among the Fianna would probably be due to ignorance. The *Book of Howth* tells us further that the Fenians waxed bold and insolent, so that the kings of Ireland banded together against them and at the battle of Arde-Kaghe the Fenians were disastrously defeated. Finn himself, being in Rome at the time, escaped; [15] but within the

---

[12] See above, pp. 29–31, for a description of the MS and the poetry in it. It is best consulted in the *Calendar of the Carew Manuscripts*, V.

[13] *Ibid.*, p. 1. On the right name and pedigree of Finn, see Kuno Meyer, "Find Mac Umaill," *Revue celtique*, (1911), 32, 391–95.

[14] *Carew MSS*, V, 2.

[15] *Ibid.*, pp. 2–6.

space of a month after the battle all the Fenians were dead "saving one man, as appeared afore was Osseyne Macke Feyn Magh Coylle in the year of our Lord 330." [16]

The story of a colloquy between St. Patrick and a Fenian hero, one of the most persistent of the legends and indicated before by Campion, crops up again. In this version it is Oisin who survives:

This Ossyon that I spake of afore was son to Fyn McKoyll, and was alive in Saint Patrick's time, which was in the year of our Savior 432. Being asked by St. Patrick what thing grieved him most, he said that he being at Hallon a night, and heard roaring of the red deer, fallow deer, the roebuck, and great number of wolves; then I remember[ed] my friends and kinsmen that pastime did use, as my father Fyn McKoyll, and the rest of Fyn Eryn. And Saint Patrick asked what Fyn McKoyll was, and what Fyn Eryn did. He answered that was hard for him to do, for he said, "Truly I think he was the best that ever was." "Say not so," said Saint Patrick; "God was the best." "Well, thou sayest that thy God knowest all, and that there is nothing but he seeth. And truly in Fyn McKoyll my father his house there would be a great number of people unknown to him; the number of his soldiers was so many, and his people; and some think he was better than thy God and master." [17]

In this earliest English version of part of the colloquy itself is the familiar and engaging defiance of Patrick by Oisin as well as Patrick's militant championing of his own God: the Christian and pagan worlds in conflict and neither yielding. But the *Book of Howth* relates that Oisin was finally converted and baptized; on the occasion of the baptism

St. Patrick having a croyge or bahell in his hand, wherein was a long prick of iron, and in saying his service at that baptism, he thought that he strake the bayghell down in the ground, and by chance he strake it through Osseyn's foot, which suffered it patiently, and after service done, a great deal of blood appeared on the ground. Saint Patrick

[16] *Carew MSS*, V, 7.
[17] *Ibid.*, p. 9.

asked Osseyn why he did not complain when he felt himself hurt. He said that he thought it was part of the baptism. He was of the age of 7 score and eight years at this time.[18]

Patrick apparently had a habit of pinning the foot of an unwary baptizee to the ground, for Keating tells a similar story of Aongus, King of Munster, and his baptism by Patrick.[19]

Among the several other tales that the *Book of Howth* says were related to the Saint by Oisin is one about Finn's guileful defeat of a giant who battles with Goll MacMorna for three days;[20] and a story of a man named Gorre who, while the Fianna were absent hunting, burned Finn's house together with many of the wives and children of the warriors. When the Fianna returned they pursued Gorre, and finally

found him in a cave, and willed his son called Hue to bring him out dead or alive. Their manner was, that he that had taken upon him his armour last should give the first charge. And so he went upon his father, not understanding in the beginning what he was, and slew him, which after made him mad. And when Fin McKoyll knew that Hue was beside his wit, he willed every of them to lie as they were dead; which did. After Hue came out, and finding them so, did throw them with his feet a certain space off, and said, "Be-like, whilst I was killing my father, these men fought a field." So he departed, and came where a herd was keeping his cattle, and he asked to fight with him, which told him that he was not a match for him, but bade him go to a wood that was by, and be avenged on that; and so did, and came again. And the herd bade him to go to the sea, and there fight his fill with the sea; and being there a while he fell asleep at the low water, lacking meat and sleep, and there was drowned. And after both he and his father was buried together.[21]

This tale is a remarkable version of a story usually associated with the Red Branch cycle: the Irish Sohrab and Rustum legend of Cuchulin's unwittingly killing his son and then, in madness

[18] *Ibid.*
[19] O'Connor's translation, pp. 332–33.
[20] *Carew MSS*, V, 8–9.
[21] *Ibid.*, pp. 7–8.

over the deed he has done, venting his battle rage on the sea. In some variants Cuchulin thus loses his life. The Red Branch story has been used several times by Yeats.[22] So far as I know, the story of Gorre and his son Hue is the only instance in which this Cuchulin story has been given as part of the Finn cycle. Only less interesting than the story itself is the vigor and straightforwardness of the prose style in which it is told.

These legends from the *Book of Howth* provided Meredith Hanmer, D.D. (1543–1603) with some of the material for his *Chronicle of Ireland*. Hanmer, mentioned briefly above,[23] was born in Shropshire, attended Christ Church College, and went to Ireland in 1591. That same year he was appointed archdeacon of Ross and vicar of Timoleague. Ware says of him that he was

made chaplain of Christ-Church College in April, 1567, took his degree in Arts, and was at length promoted to the vicarage of St. Leonard's, Shore-ditch, London. He left behind him there . . . an ill name among his parishioners for converting the Brass of several antient Monuments into Coin.[24]

In 1593 he was made treasurer of Waterford Cathedral, and by 1603 had risen to the chancellorship of the Cathedral Church of St. Canice in Kilkenny.[25] His chronicle was first published by Ware in 1633 and was republished by the Hibernian Press Society in 1809.[26] It is a history of Ireland from its legendary beginnings to the middle of the thirteenth century.

Hanmer takes his legends from the *Book of Howth* with very

[22] The story is used in *On Baile's Strand,* London, 1904; part of it in "Cuchulain's Fight with the Sea," *Collected Poems,* pp. 37–41. This last-named was originally called "The Death of Cuchullin," and appeared in *The Countess Kathleen and Various Legends and Lyrics,* London, 1892.

[23] P. 26.

[24] Harris, ed., *The Whole Works of Sir James Ware Concerning Ireland,* II, 2, 328.

[25] *DNB.*

[26] Ware, ed., *op. cit.,* Dublin, 1809. Vol. I has Spenser and Campion; Vol. II has Hanmer and Marleburrough.

little change, but he does make additions. For example, after giving the genealogy of Finn he goes on and works up an ingenious etymology for "Erin." He says:

For proof of this historie [Finn's ancestry], I finde in *Saxo Grammaticus* that wrote the historie of the Danes, that Fin and Finni were a great sept there, hardy, stalworth men, given to preying, and burning of towne and country, and happly the Irish conversing with them did learne those parts of them and that the name of Eric was of royall bloud among them; [27] so Fin Erin turning *c*. into *n*. was a great commander there, and conducted into Ireland many Danes. And happly, Ireland of old, because of his great command, and his posteritie, might after him be called Erin: this is but my conceit, happly others can say more thereof.[28]

And elsewhere he gives a picture that has become traditional of an island people on the watch against invasion. The chief commanders of the Fianna, by direction from "Fin Mac Koyll . . . tooke farther order that Beacons should be set up in sundry places of the land, where in time of danger they might have direction for reliefe, and draw to a head for their defense." [29] Toward the close of his life Finn evidently fell on evil days. ". . . the end of Fin Mac Coill was, that he dyed a beggar and in great miserie. So farre out of the booke of Houth." [30] This last statement of Hanmer's is not correct according to the make-up of the *Book of Howth* today, for neither of the two quotations given immediately above appears in it.

Hanmer's famous contemporary, Edmund Spenser (1552–99), was apparently not interested particularly in Irish history or legend, since his *View of the Present State of Ireland* deals for the most part with the living conditions of the people. He has some interest for us, however, because he had enough curiosity

[27] Hanmer probably refers to Saxo's description of the Finns and Erik of Sweden's invasion. See Elton and Powell, *The First Nine Books of* . . . *Saxo Grammaticus*, Folk-lore Society Publications, XXXIII, 203–4.

[28] Hanmer, *op. cit.*, p. 45.

[29] *Ibid.*, p. 53.

[30] *Ibid.*, p. 63.

about the native literature to have translations of some Gaelic poems made for him; and because he was, as far as I know, the first Englishman living in Ireland to have anything good to say for Gaelic poetry. Spenser went to Ireland as secretary to Lord Grey de Wilton, the lord deputy, in 1580. He became one of the "undertakers" for the settlement of Munster in 1586, and acquired Kilcolman castle in county Cork. The two years from 1589 to 1591 he spent in London, returning reluctantly to Kilcolman in the latter year. He was in London again in 1596, where at the home of the Earl of Essex he wrote the *View*. In 1597 he returned to Kilcolman for the last time; in 1598 the castle was burnt during an insurrection of the O'Neills under the leadership of the Earl of Desmond, and Spenser and his family fled first to Cork and then to London where he died in want.[31]

That Spenser held the common Elizabethan prejudice toward Ireland is surprising in view of his long opportunity to study the country at first hand. Yet one has only to read the *View* to find a distaste and hatred of the native Irish and their customs even more marked than in the work of many lesser men. And even in the favorable notice he gave the native poetry he found a fancied reason for tempering his words.

I have caused divers of them [Gaelic poems] to be translated unto me that I might understand them: and surely they savoured of sweet wit and good invention, but skilled not of the goodly ornaments of poetry: yet were they sprinkled with some pretty flowers of their naturall desire which gave good grace and comeliness unto them, the which it is a great pity to see abused, to the gracing of wickedness and vice, which with good usage would serve to adorne and beautifie virtue.[32]

Unfortunately these translations have not survived so we cannot tell in what way the Gaelic poets graced "wickedness and vice" with their poetry.

A few years after Spenser's death, Florence MacCarthy (1563–

---

[31] *DNB.*

[32] *The Works of Spenser,* ed. Collier, V, 387.

1640), a prominent Irish political figure during the latter years of Elizabeth's reign, in a letter in English [33] to Conor O'Brien, Earl of Thomond, drew up an epitome of Irish history from the mythical period to Strongbow's arrival. MacCarthy's letter was apparently written from the Tower of London, where because of "treasonable" activities he was confined off and on for almost the last forty years of his life.[34] His epitome has some value in the evidence it presents us with of the seventeenth-century Anglo-Irishman's curiosity about the early history of Ireland. And evidence that the saga stories were very much a part of the average Irishman's background is shown by MacCarthy's finding room in his epitome for a paragraph about them:

Then had they those that were called *curidha* (heroes) as *Curi, Conall, Cernach, Cuchulin,* and others that for their agility, strength, and activity and valour were much celebrated: and about one hundred and fifty years later they had those bands or companies called *fiena* that for their activity and valour were elected and chosen out of all the provinces. Their chief charge was to watch all the havens, and keep the country from sudden invasion, being commanded by *Cumhaill mac Trenmoir,* a Leinsterman, and by Finn mac Cumhaill, his son, after he was killed at the battle of Cnuca by *Conn Cedcathach,* or Counn (of the hundred battles).[35]

MacCarthy's epitome did not involve any direct translation from Gaelic manuscript sources; nor, for that matter, have any of the fragments of the old stories that we have found so far in English. The first such translation seems to have been that of Conall Mageoghegan, who in 1627 put into English the *Annals of Clonmacnoise,* annals of Ireland from the earliest period to 1408. Mageoghegan, Irish historian and scribe, settled at Lismoyn, county Westmeath, where he did most of his work. Very

[33] Standish Hayes O'Grady, *Catalogue of Irish Manuscripts in the British Museum,* I, 61–62 (addit. MS 4793, ff. 21, 22).
[34] Sir John T. Gilbert, ed., *Facsimiles of National Manuscripts of Ireland,* Pt. IV. Vol. I., introduction, pp. lxviii–lxxiii.
[35] *Ibid.,* appendix, p. 122. The whole epitome is on pp. 120–23.

little else is known of him.[36] His translation was published by
Denis Murphy in 1896.[37] We do not know, of course, how widely
Mageoghegan's work circulated in manuscript or how many
copies were made of it. The original manuscript is lost, and
there are but three extant copies.[38]

What we have of the Red Branch and Finn cycles in the *Annals of Clonmacnoise* is not great in quantity but it makes more
distinct and familiar the figures that we have up to now been
able only to outline or to mention. So far, all we have learned
of the heroes of the Red Branch or their stories are the name
"Kokoyllon," that I have suggested may be a misspelling for
Cuchulin; the tale of Gorre, incorrectly placed in the Finn cycle
or else an analogue of the Red Branch story of Cuchulin's killing his son: both of these from the *Book of Howth;* and the
names Conall, Cernach, and Cuchullain in MacCarthy's epitome.[39] Now we can add a little to our scanty Red Branch material: first, from the following paragraph about Cuchulin:

Cowchoullen the Heroicke Champion of Ireland and Heber his Wife
Dyed. The Champion was killed by the sons of Calletin of Connaught
in the 27th yeare of his age. The Report goes that he killed a Ravenous
and uenemous Dogg when he was but the age of 7 yeares & was alsoe
but of the age of 17 yeares when he surpassed all the Champions in
Ireland in the Disention between them for the famous prey called in
Irish tane Boe Cwailgne.[40]

Next, an interesting character sketch of Maeve, the doughty
queen of Connaught and leader, during the Red Branch days,
of the warriors who fought against the Ultonian knights:

yt famous (but not altogether for Goodness) woman Meaw Crwa-
chan, [who was notorious] because of her great boldness, Buty, & stout

---

[36] *DNB.*

[37] For the Royal Society of Antiquaries, Dublin.

[38] One in the British Museum; one in Trinity College Library, Dublin; and
one in Lord Drogheda's library at Monasterevan, co. Kildare. See Murphy's
introduction and *DNB* article on Mageoghegan.

[39] See above, pp. 63, 64–65, 69.

[40] Denis Murphy, ed. *The Annals of Clonmacnoise,* p. 48.

manlyness in Giving of battles, insatiable Lust, her father allowed her for her portion the province of Connaught, & shee made an oath never to marry with anyone whatsoever that would be stayned with any of these 3 Defects and Imperfections as she accoumpted them vidzt with jealousy for any Letchery that she should committ, with unmanliness or Imbecillitie, soe as the party could not be soe bould as to undertake any adventure whatsoever were it never soe Dificult, & Lastly she would never marry with anyone that feared any man liveing.[41]

And the ancient chronicler told also the story of the building of Emain Macha, the capital of Ulster; a story that concerns Queen Macha, whose throne was threatened in a war with five brothers. After defeating the army of the brothers, the Queen goes in pursuit of them alone and in disguise. She comes on them at nightfall as they are seated around a fire at their evening meal; when the eldest asks her to slip away with him into a thicket she agrees. Once there she overpowers and binds him; she repeats the performance with the others. After she has marched them back to her capital she forces them to build her a new palace, that she calls Emain Macha, that became the dwelling-place of the Ulster kings.[42]

From the material dealing with Finn in *The Annals of Clonmacnoise*, we have the first English account of the tests a recruit had to pass to be accepted into the Fianna, tests that are essentially the same as those Lady Gregory gives in her *Gods and Fighting Men* (1904):

Finn mcCoyle als O'Boysgne the great hunter, Cheef head of all the K's forces in Ireland and Defender of the Kingdom from foraine invaders was Beheaded by Aihleagh mcDurgrean and by the sonns of Wirgrean of the lordship of Lwyne of Tarah at Athbrea on the river of Boyne. This Finn had under his leading 7 great Cohorts of very huge and tall biggness. None was excepted into any of the Cohorts untill he had Learned out the 12 Irish Books of poetry & could

[41] *Ibid.*, p. 47.
[42] *Ibid.*, pp. 39-40.

say them without booke, if the Party to be excepted would defend
himself with his targett & sword from 9 throwes of Dartes of 9 of the
Company that would stand but 9 Ridges from him at distance, and
either cut the Dartes with his sword or Receave them all on his targett without Bleeding on him he would be accepted, otherwise not,
if the party running through the thickest woods of Ireland were over-
taken by any of the seven Cohorts they all pursueing him with all
their might and maine he would not be taken of them in their Company. But if he had out-Runned them all without loss of any haire
of his head; without Breaking any ould stick under his feet & leping
over any tree as yt he should meet, as high as the top of his head
without Impediment, and stooping under a tree as low as his knee
& taking a thorne out of his foot (if it should chance to be in) with
his naile without Impediment of his Running; all of which if he had
Don, he would be excepted as one of the Company, otherwise not,
this Finn his Dwelling place was Allon in Leinster, he had many
sonns and Daughters as Ossyn macFinn, Aydan mcFinn, & c. hee
had another Dwelling town called Moyelly in Meath, wch is now
called Foxes countrey, he was very Learned, wise & a great Prophett.
He prophesyed of the coming of the Englishmen into this land, with
many other things.[43]

Almost fifty years elapsed after Mageoghegan's translation
before there were any further English versions of Irish legends
or English translations of Gaelic poetry. But the work of Geoffrey Keating, the greatest of early Irish historians, was finished
in Gaelic during the first half of the seventeenth century, and
Keating's work was to form much of the basis of Peter Walsh's
*A Prospect of the State of Ireland from the Year of the World
1756 to the Year of Christ 1652,* published in London in 1682.

Peter Walsh (1618?–88), an Irish Franciscan educated at
Louvain, was one of the most prominent political-religious
figures of his day; at one time he was chaplain to Lord Castle-
haven at whose suggestion he published his history.[44] Walsh in

[43] Denis Murphy, ed. *The Annals of Clonmacnoise,* pp. 61–62. Cf. Lady
Gregory's *Gods and Fighting Men,* London, 1904, pp. 169–70.
[44] *DNB.*

his preface cites authorities he has read: Cambrensis, Campion, Hanmer, Spenser, as well as the Gaelic historians and chroniclers, especially Keating. "In short," he says, "when I was a young man I had read Geoffrey Keating's Irish Manuscript History of Ireland"; [45] and he proceeds to give a brief outline of that history.[46] The legends told by Keating, however, are not much thought of by Walsh; he mentions nothing of the Red Branch stories, and what he has to say of the Finn cycle he tries to put on solid ground:

As to their constant ordinary Militia, what it was in their times of peace we find in the reign of *Cormock Ulfada* (the son of Airt) King of *Ireland* a little after the birth of *Christ*. For then it consisted of three Battalions or Divisions, of equal number each, in all nine thousand men, under several Commanders, and Fionn mhac Cuual their General; who was neither Gyant, nor Dane, nor other Foreigner, as no more were any of his Commanders, Captains or Souldiers. He was himself but of the ordinary stature of other men . . . and he was an *Irish* man both by birth and descent lineally come, of his Mothers side, in the fifth Generation, from Nuatha Neacht King of *Leinster*, and so upward all along from Herimon; whatever is reported by *D. Hanmer* to the contrary . . . *Hanmer* might as well have made the *Cappadocian* Knight a *Saxon*, as Fionn the son of Cuual, a Dane. And so might *Hector Boethius* have as well turned *Huon* of Bordeaux, or *Amadis de Gaul*, or the *Knight of the Sun*, or the *Seven Champions of Christendom*, and such like Romances into the very truest Histories, as the Fables written of *Fiona Erionn*, only to entertain leasurable hours and Fancy . . . In short, these Gentlemen *Fionn mhac Cuul* and *Fiona Erionn* were the stoutest and bravest fighting men of their time in *Ireland*. And they were kept in constant pay by the Monarch, Princes, and people of that Kingdom, to guard the coasts from abroad, and keep all at home quiet . . . And this is the naked truth concerning these *Fiona Erionn* so famous in their Generation. On which truth many fabulous stories have been superstructed.[47]

[45] *A Prospect of the State of Ireland*, p. 16.
[46] *Ibid.*, pp. 17–29.
[47] *Ibid.*, pp. 51–53.

Of much interest in this quotation is the light that it throws on the way in which the legend of Finn had assumed truth in the mind of the educated Irishman; even an Irishman of such catholic tastes in his reading as Walsh shows himself to be.

So far as I could discover, Walsh's *Prospect* made no great stir in its time; and it apparently has always been, as have Walsh's other works, a fairly rare and hard-to-obtain volume.[48] Sir Richard Cox in his *Hibernia Anglicana* (1689) [49] is one of the few who takes any notice of it. And Cox, an Irish judge and strong Protestant, who was lord chancellor from 1703 to 1707,[50] has nothing kind to say of either Walsh or Keating.[51] Nor is he kinder to Ireland's tales from legend and mythology; he assails the "ridiculous stories which they have published of the Firbolgs and Tuah-de-danans." [52]

---

[48] *DNB*, life of Walsh.
[49] London.
[50] *DNB*.
[51] Cox, *op. cit.*, introduction, pp. 1–2.
[52] *Ibid.*, "An Apparatus," p. 4.

Molyneux, Swift, and MacCurtin

THE last part of the seventeenth century and the first two decades of the eighteenth century are marked by no specific works pertinent to our study. But the activities of two men— William Molyneux and Jonathan Swift—during these years should be noted. Both had a profound and direct influence on Irish nationalism, and when a land is swept by a wave of nationalism its people instinctively turn to a study and idealization of their country's past.

Molyneux (1656–98) was born in Dublin and graduated from Trinity College, Dublin, in 1675. He was of the gentleman class and had enough money to gratify his varied interests. In 1680 he published in London an English translation of Descartes' *Meditations*. Of direct concern here, he "was instrumental in forming [in 1683] a Society in Dublin similar to the Royal Society in London, of which he was an illustrious member . . but . . . the distracted state of the kingdom dispersed [the society] as soon as 1688." [53] The society formed by Molyneux was known as the Dublin Philosophical Society and had as its purpose inquiries into the antiquities of Ireland. Molyneux' contributions were mainly scientific; [54] other members, however, read papers from time to time dealing with certain aspects of ancient Ireland. The society renewed its activity in 1707 [55] for a

[53] Ronert Burrowes, preface, *Transactions of the Royal Irish Academy*, I (1787), p. xiii.

[54] Samuel Ayscough, *op. cit.*, I, 473, MS 4811: "Minutes and Register of the Philosophical Society of Dublin, from 1683, to 1687, with copies of the papers read before them." Molyneux' contributions are listed on pp. 473–74 and are as follows: 1) Concerning Lough-Neagh, and its petrifying quality; 2) A way of viewing pictures in miniature; 3) Queries relating to Lough Neagh.

[55] *Ibid.*, p. 476, MS 4812: "Register of the Philosophical Society of Dublin, from August 14, 1707, with copies of some of the papers."

short time; ultimately it was to be looked back on as the precursor of the Royal Irish Academy that was founded in 1786.[56]

In 1692 Molyneux was returned as M.P. for Dublin University and he was still sitting in 1698 when he wrote his famous essay, *The Case of Ireland's Being Bound by Acts of Parliament Made in England*.[57] It is not surprising that the English ordered all available copies burned in the palace yard in Dublin, for it was to be many years before Englishmen stopped looking askance at Irishmen who had the temerity to stand up for their country. But Molyneux' pamphlet circulated widely; it pointed the way to eventual independence.

The name of Jonathan Swift (1667–1745) was coupled with that of Molyneux by Henry Grattan in his memorable speech to the Irish Parliament on April 16, 1782, when he introduced a motion for a Declaration of Rights: "Spirit of Swift! Spirit of Molyneux! Your genius has prevailed." [58] During Swift's tenure as dean of St. Patrick's in Dublin from 1713 to his death in 1745, he was constantly agitating in favor of the Irish. His pamphlets for the Irish cause began in 1720 with "A Proposal for the Universal Use of Irish Manufacture" and continued intermittently until very near the end of his life. They included the famous *Drapier's Letters* of 1724 that put the quietus on the notorious minting scheme of William Wood; and that high-water mark of satire, "A Modest Proposal for preventing the Children of Poor People from being a Burden to their Parents or the Country," written in 1729.

Besides this encouragement of the spirit of Irish nationalism, Swift in at least one poem, "The Description of an Irish Feast," written in 1720, touches the field of translation of Gaelic poetry into English. The poem is based on a Gaelic original, "Plearaca na Ruarcach," attributed to Hugh MacGawran, a Gaelic poet who flourished during the early years of the eighteenth century.

[56] Burrowes, *op. cit.*, p. xiv.
[57] *DNB.*
[58] Eleanor Hull, *A History of Ireland*, II, 220.

According to one story, Swift was given by MacGawran himself a literal English translation, and it was from this translation that Swift composed.[59]

The Gaelic poem "Pléaraca na Ruarcach" is believed to celebrate a great feast given by O'Rourke, a powerful Ulster chieftain during the reign of Elizabeth, when he left on a visit to Her Majesty.[60] Swift's poem is in dimeter measure, with the feet a mixture of iambus and anapaest. Its rousing swing can best be appreciated from a brief example:

> O'Rourk's noble Fare
> Will ne'er be forgot,
> By those who were there
> Or those who were not.
> His revels to keep,
> We sup and we dine,
> On seven Score Sheep
> Fat Bullocks and Swine.[61]

A curious and interesting epilogue to the story of O'Rourke's visit to the Queen is told by Joseph Cooper Walker in his *Historical Memoirs of the Irish Bards* (1786). According to Walker, this tale "wanders about the county of Leitrim"; it says that when O'Rourke arrived at court the Queen, much impressed by his handsome figure, gave him elaborate quarters in the palace. To these quarters a mysterious lady came night after night, leaving always a little before dawn. All efforts of the puzzled warrior to learn the identity of his visitor were repulsed; one moonlight night, however, he noticed on one of her fingers an intricately jeweled ring. He saw what he took to be the same ring on one of the Queen's fingers the next day and was foolish enough to speak to her about it. That night, instead of the lady, a swordsman came, and O'Rourke paid for his rashness with his

---

[59] Harold Williams, *The Poems of Jonathan Swift*, I, 243–44.
[60] Sir Walter Scott, *The Works of Jonathan Swift*, 2nd ed., XIV, 130.
[61] Williams, *op. cit.*, I, 244.

life.[62] So far the tale; as a matter of historic fact, O'Rourke of
Leitrim was handed over to Elizabeth by James VI of Scotland
and executed in London in November, 1591.

"The Description of an Irish Feast," in Swift's version, does
not give a very flattering picture of life at the home of an Irish
chieftain; but it is gone one better by a coarse satire published
in London in 1724 called sometimes "Gillo's Feast," though
more commonly known as *Hesperi-neso-graphia,* or the Western Isle described, by William Moffet. It is not unlikely that
Swift's poem inspired the writing of *Hesperi-neso-graphia.* The
eight cantos of iambic tetrameter couplets of the latter poem
show in scenes of almost unbelievable cheapness and vulgarity
what Moffet, whoever he was,[63] imagined the entertainment
customs of the native Irish to be. Why Sir Samuel Ferguson
called Moffet's poem "Irish literature" is hard to say: it is·neither
"Irish" nor "literature." [64]

Swift belongs properly, of course, to English literature; yet
it is hard to underestimate the influence he had on Irish literature by helping to force the flame of Irish nationalism. As has
been pointed out above, that nationalism must have had as one
of its results the sending of the people to a closer study of their
country's past, including its legends and literature. For of no
country can it be said so truly as it can be said of Ireland that
politics and literature tend to go hand in hand. So it has been
from the time of the bards who sang their chieftains into battle,
and mourned them when they did not come back.

Thus it may not be without significance that Swift was dean
of St. Patrick's and was writing his pro-Irish pamphlets, and
the words of Molyneux were echoing over the land, when Hugh
MacCurtin in 1717 composed his *Brief Discourse of the Antiquity of Ireland* and Dermod O'Connor in 1723 published his

[62] London, pp. 81–82.

[63] D. J. O'Donoghue, *Poets of Ireland,* p. 311, thinks William Moffet was a
pseudonym for Walter Jones.

[64] *Dublin University Magazine,* IX (1837), 546–58.

translation of Geoffrey Keating's *Foras Feasa Ar Eirinn* (A General History of Ireland).

Hugh MacCurtin (1680?–1755), Irish antiquary and Gaelic poet, was educated in France, where for seven years he was a tutor in the Dauphin's household. He returned to Ireland in 1714. Besides books in Gaelic, he wrote an English-Gaelic dictionary that was published at Paris in 1732.[65] His *Brief Discourse* is important for a number of reasons. In the first place, he felt there was some necessity of writing in English even though he says, "I confess my self not sufficient to write correctly in the English Language"; [66] hence, there must have been a demand for such a book among the English-speaking Irish. In the second place, he gives us for the first time in English hints of the Deirdre story: it occurs in his discussion of the reign of Conchobar where there is likewise a somewhat mixed-up reference to the Tain bo Cualgne:

The ruin of the Posterity of Ir happen'd in this Monarch's Reign: For Feargus Grandson to the Monarch Rughruidhe the Great, being incens'd against Conor then King of Ulster . . . he came first to the Monarch Eochaidh, and crav'd aid against Conor: the Monarch not only promis'd him his Friendship, but also gave him several Gifts in Token of his Favour. Feargus took a strong Party of Armed Men along with him into Ulster, and burnt and destroy'd a great part of that Country, and brought a great Prey to Lenster. Conor seeing how fatal the discord which happen'd between him and his Cousin Feargus was to his Country; he sent his own Brother, a wise and valiant Man, by name Cabhthach, to Feargus, and promis'd, or offer'd him the one half of the Province to be in Peace and Unity with him, as formerly, which Feargus accepted. But a few years after, a much greater difference happen'd between them about the brave Champions Clann Uisneach, i.e. the Sons or Children of Uisneach their own Cousins, who were murder'd by Conor's wicked contrivance.[67]

---

[65] *DNB.*
[66] *A Brief Discourse in Vindication of the Antiquity of Ireland*, p. ix.
[67] *Ibid.*, pp. 79–80.

Because of this murder, Fergus destroys Emain and four of Conchobar's sons; Cormac Conloingas goes with Fergus to Connaught to Maeve's court where Fergus "made Courtship to the Queen . . . and . . . got on her three Sons, viz. Ciar, Corc, and Conmhac." [68] For seven hundred years, MacCurtin says, "the Champions of Ulster were the most renowned for Valour and Strength in all the western Parts of Europe." [69]

What material he has about Finn and the Fianna is almost word for word from Peter Walsh's *Prospect,* though he adds a paragraph about the requirements for getting into the Fianna.

No Man was receiv'd into this Army or Militia, but such as should perform ten Conditions, that none cou'd possibly do, but such as had a Store of Strength, Courage, Valour, and Agility, almost incredible to be in any human Body. [70]

Of far greater importance than MacCurtin's work, however, is Dermod O'Connor's translation of Geoffrey Keating's *Foras Feasa Ar Eirinn,* for that translation contains the most complete account of Irish legend in English we have from any of the early Irish historians: Keating, through his translator, is to Irish literature what Geoffrey of Monmouth is to English literature.

[68] *A Brief Discourse in Vindication of the Antiquity of Ireland,* pp. 80–81.
[69] *Ibid.,* p. 82.
[70] *Ibid.,* p. 114.

❧ 4 ❧

Keating and Dermod O'Connor

GEOFFREY KEATING was born about 1570 in Tipperary, near the
village of Burgess. He was educated first at home and then for
twenty years studied abroad, returning to his native land as an
ordained priest. He gained wide popularity as a preacher in the
south of Ireland; but after delivering a fiery sermon on adultery
that was taken too personally by a lady of his audience who was
on terms of intimacy with the lord president of Munster, Sir
George Carew, he fled to escape arrest. The remainder of his
life Keating wandered throughout the length and breadth of
Ireland reading and studying old books and manuscripts, many
of which were destroyed or lost in the wars and "troubles" that
came about soon after his death. He is thought to have completed his history about 1640 and to have died about 1644. His
work was "one of the best known of Irish books till the final
decay of literature [that is, Gaelic literature] after the famine
of 1846, and the last book of importance to circulate in the
British Isles in manuscript." [71]

English translations of Keating's history have been numerous.
The earliest mention of a translation I have found is in Peter
Walsh's *Prospect* (1682). Walsh, in speaking of Keating's history in his preface and of the fact that he had read it in Irish
when he was a young man, goes on to say that "And now . . .
I remembered how about four or five years since, the R. H. Earl
of Anglesey, Lord Privy Seal, had been pleas'd to show me another Manuscript, being an English Translation of that Irish
History of Keatings." [72] Walsh does not further identify this

[71] *DNB.* A good estimate of Keating is in Thomas J. Shahan's "An Irish
Historian of the Seventeenth Century," *American Catholic Quarterly Review,*
XXVIII (April 1914), 310–38.
[72] Peter Walsh, *op. cit.,* preface, p. 16.

translation; it may have been Michael Kearney's, first noticed in John Daly's preface to Daly's edition of *The Kings of the Race of Eibhear* (Dublin, 1847), a translation of a Gaelic poem by Kearney. Daly speaks of the translation of Keating in these words:

That which I now present to the reader [the translation of *The Kings of the Race of Eibhear*] I found in an unpublished manuscript translation of Dr. Keating's *Foras Feasa Ar Eirinn;* made by a celebrated scribe Michael Kearney, of Ballyloskye, in the County of Crosse Tipperary; who, being a contemporary of his learned author, began the task, A.D. 1635, which he brought to a successful close in 1668; it . . . is now in the hands of a gentleman in this city.

(If Daly is correct in his dates, Kearney must have started his translation before Keating was finished.) Sir John T. Gilbert, in the *Facsimiles of National Manuscripts of Ireland,* includes a plate of Kearney's translation,[73] and as far as I know this is the only time any of it has been published.

Another translation is noted by T. K. Abbot and E. J. Gwynn in their *Catalogue of Irish Manuscripts in the Library of Trinity College:* "Keating's History of Ireland translated into English. Transcribed by Humphrey Moynihan and Thomas Moynihan. Purchased from Thomas Moynihan near Killarney, by Edward Llwyd, A.D. 1700." [74] Still another is spoken of by Theophilus O'Flanagan, who in a paper read before the Royal Irish Academy in 1786 recalled a translation by the eighteenth-century Gaelic poet Michael Comyn, who "was celebrated for his knowledge of Irish antiquities. He made a translation of Keating, which he intended to publish, but death prevented the execu-

---

[73] Pt. IV. (PL. LXXIII. *History of Ireland* by Geoffrey Keating. Trin. Coll. Commencement of Preface, transcr. by John O'Maelchonaire. Text and transl. PL. LXXIV. Michael Kearney's English Version, 1668. Irish & English.) London, 1882.

[74] #1443 H. 2. 14, p. 322.

tion of his design, and the manuscript has since been fatally lost." [75]

Walter Harris, in his edition of Ware, mentions two translations:

I have in my custody a Manuscript Copy of a Translation of this work [Keating's history], done by another Hand; but . . . much inferior to Mr. O'Connor's; yet it appears from it, that Mr. O'Connor hath taken an unjustifiable Liberty in abridging his author's work in some particulars, or this other Translator, on the contrary hath been too bold in enlarging it.[76]

Harris gives no hint of the name—he probably did not know it —of the "other Translator." David Comyn, in the preface to his translation for the Irish Texts Society, mentions what he thinks is the "other Translator's" work: "there is . . . an English translation much abridged, and rather vague and inaccurate, in manuscript (date about 1700); to this, perhaps, it is that Harris refers in his edition of Ware." [77]

The "Mr. O'Connor" that Harris does mention, however, is the most important of the early translators of Keating, for his was the only translation published until the early nineteenth century. That it was widely read there can be little doubt, for a second edition folio appeared in 1726—only three years after the first edition folio of 1723—and a third edition folio in 1738. The subscribers to the first edition numbered over three hundred.[78] Later editions appeared in 1809, 1841, and 1857.

Nothing is known of Dermod O'Connor. He was probably something of a rogue, for in a note in the appendix of the third

[75] "An Account of an antient Inscription in Ogam Character on the Sepulchral Monument of an Irish Chief," *Transactions Royal Irish Academy*, I (1787), section "Antiquities," 7.

[76] Harris, ed., *op. cit.*, II, 2, 106.

[77] Irish Texts Society, IV, ix.

[78] Geoffrey Keating, *The General History of Ireland*, translated by Dermod O'Connor. The list follows the preface.

edition, B. Creake, the bookseller, says that O'Connor had absconded with three hundred pounds of subscribers' money that belonged rightfully to him, Creake.[79]

From time to time critical notices of O'Connor's work appeared. William Nicholson, in the *Irish Historical Library* (1724), intimates that it caused something of a furore:

... it [Keating's history] seems to have wanted a review before it appeared abroad. This it has now done in a comely dress; and Mr. O'Connor, the translator and publisher, an Irish Antiquary by descent, appears to be a Person well able to do right to his Author and himself: Notwithstanding the many hard censures that have pass'd, and are daily passing, upon both.[80]

Charles O'Conor, in his *Dissertations on the History of Ireland* (1753), was harder on his namesake:

It is but justice ... to inform the Reader, that his [Keating's] pretended Translator has hardly rendered him Justice, in a single Period, through the whole Work. The History given in English, under Keating's name, is the grossest Imposition that has been ever yet obtruded on a learned age.[81]

The censures were echoed by the later translators [82] of Keating, but whatever garblings of translation O'Connor made are not evident in his lively, concrete English. And, as far as we are concerned here, the poor quality of his scholarship could in no wise lessen the knowledge of Irish legend that reached the English-speaking Irish from his work. Everyone seemed to know it. In 1777, for instance, John Watkinson, M.D., an Englishman

[79] London, 1738, p. xv.

[80] Dublin, p. 46.

[81] Preface, p. x.

[82] John O'Mahony, who published a translation in New York in 1857, says in the preface, p. 5: "Upon comparing some manuscript copies of the *Foras Feasa Ar Eirinn* with the previously published translation, Dermod O'Connor's English was found so unlike what Dr. Keating actually wrote"; and David Comyn, in the preface, pp. viii–ix, Vol. I, of his translation, speaks of "Dermod O'Connor's unsatisfactory translation."

traveling in Ireland, remarks in a letter to a friend apropos of a discussion of the writers of Ireland, that "the fabulous Keating is well known to everybody." [83] Joseph Ritson, in 1783, bases a discussion of the Irish bards and their troubles on Keating.[84] And as late as 1880, Edward Arber, in the introduction to his edition of Stanihurst's *Aeneid,* quotes from "G. Keating, D.D. in his *General History of Ireland,* p. xii. Ed. 1723." the reasons Keating gives for Stanihurst's being unfitted to write a chronicle of Ireland.[85]

Keating's stories from legend are, as I have said above, by far the most complete to his time, and were a storehouse of material from which later writers drew freely. (When in the following account of the legendary material of Keating I use his name, it is understood that I refer to O'Connor's translation.) Not only is there a great deal of the Red Branch and the Finn cycles, but there is also a goodly sprinkling of other tales. Keating was not a man to let a good story go untold. His anecdote, for example, about the wife of Partholanus, which gentleman was Ireland's first inhabitant, is almost Chaucerian, and as a case of anticlimax is almost beyond compare.

Partholanus's wife, says Keating, had a favorite greyhound named Samer; when the greyhound died on a certain island, Partholanus named the island Inis Samer. Incidentally, Partholanus himself killed the dog in a rage because "of the loose Behaviour of his Wife" who prostituted herself to one of her footmen. When her husband expostulated with her

she returned him this impudent Answer, "What could you otherwise expect? if you are so serv'd you must thank yourself; for set Honey by a young Girl, or sweet Milk by a Child, or Meat by a Cat, or edg'd Tools by a Carpenter, or a poor weak Woman with a brisk young Fellow in private, and on my Word they won't long be asunder. . . ."

[83] *A Philosophical Survey of the South of Ireland,* p. 416.
[84] *A Select Collection of English Songs,* I, xxxvi–xxxviii.
[85] *The English Scholar's Library* . . . #10, p. xiv.

Partholanus astonish'd at this audacious Reply, in a Fit of Passion seiz'd upon her favourite Greyhound, and threw it with all his force upon the Ground, and it died upon the Spot. . . . This is the first Instance of Jealousy and Female Falsehood in the Irish History.[86]

Keating gives also a version of the legend that tells how the palace of Emain Macha got its name,

from a Woman so called, who . . . was obliged . . . to run a Race with the Horses of Connor, King of Ulster, and . . . she out-ran them, and came first to the Goal; she was with Child at this Time, and near her Delivery; and when she fell in Labour, she was delivered of Twins, a Son and a Daughter. The Barbarity of this Action, and the Pains she suffered in Travail, so incensed the unfortunate Woman, that she left a Curse upon the Men of Ulster, and Heaven heard her; for the Men of that Province were constantly afflicted with the Pains of Child-bearing for many years, from the Time of Connor, who then reigned in Ulster. . . .[87]

These pains were what kept all the men of Ulster, save Cuchulin, debilitated when Maeve marched into Cooley on her great cattle raid.[88]

As the basic reason for the wars between Ulster and Connaught, Keating correctly names the murder of the three sons of Usnach, and he is thereby led to tell the story of Deirdre. His is the first complete account of that most famous of Irish legends, and hence is important enough to call for full treatment. He introduces it by saying that while Maeve was queen of Connaught,

there arose a most unhappy Difference between her Subjects and the Inhabitants of Ulster over which Province Connor was then King. This Contest broke out into open Hostilities, and occasioned a long War; but to give a particular Relation of these Occurrences, I am obliged to trace the Account of them to the very Beginning, and par-

---

[86] O'Connor's translation, London, 1723, pp. 24–25.

[87] *Ibid.,* pp. 156–57.

[88] See Lady Gregory, *Cuchulain of Muirthemne,* 4th ed., London, 1911, 1915, pp. 184–86.

ticularly take notice of the Death of the three Sons of Uisneach, which was the true Cause that gave Birth to these fatal Commotions.[89]

He then tells the story of Deirdre.

Connor was at an entertainment in the house of Feidhlim, son of Doill, secretary of state to Connor. During the entertainment Feidhlim's wife was delivered of a daughter. The king's druid foretold that from the child would come great disturbances. Thereupon the nobles called for her death, but Connor opposed them and sent the girl Deirdre to a strong fortress under care of Leabharcham, a "great Poetess" who could deliver

extempore Verses upon any Subject . . . It happened upon a time as Deirdre and her Governess were looking out of a Window, they spied one of the Slaughtermen of the Garrison killing a Calf for the use of her Table upon a snowy day, and some of the blood they observed fell upon the Snow, and a Raven came and fed upon it. This sight occasioned a strange Passion in the young Lady; for notwithstanding her Confinement she was of a very amorous Disposition; and turning to Leabharcham, Oh, says she, that I could be so happy as to be in the arms of a Man who was of the three Colours I now see, I mean, who had a skin as white as the driven Snow, Hair as shining black as the feathers of a Raven, and a blooming Red in his Cheeks as deep as the Calf's Blood.

Her governess, surprised, says that there is such a young man of the court, named Naoise, and Deirdre begs her governess to bring him to the fortress. And acceding to her request, Leabharcham goes to Naoise and puts the proposal before him, praising Deirdre's beauty the while, and Naoise consents.

The lovers meet, and Deirdre makes Naoise promise to elope with her. Accordingly, with his brothers Ainle and Ardan and one hundred and fifty followers, Naoise surprises the garrison and capturing Deirdre flees to Scotland. The king of that country receives them hospitably, but when he hears of the beauty of Deirdre he determines to force her from the arms of her husband into his own. Naoise learns of the plan in time, and after

[89] O'Connor, *op. cit.,* p. 175.

many skirmishes with the forces of the king manages to flee
with his companions to an island, from whence he sends for
help to his friends in Ireland.

His request was so favorably received, that the principal nobility of
the Province interceded with King Connor that they should be re-
lieved, and have liberty to return to their own Country; for they said
that it would be barbarous to suffer the three sons of Uisneach to be
destroyed on account of a lewd Woman.

So the king consented to their return, and ostensibly for-
gave the lovers; Fergus MacRoigh and Cormac Conloingias, the
king's son, are sent as envoys and guarantees of safekeeping for
the exiles; they all return but are met shortly after their landing
in Ireland by Eogan, one of Connor's hirelings, who slays the
three brothers treacherously and carries Deirdre to the court of
the king. But she is inconsolable for her dead lover, and after
hearing her weeping for a year, the "King was moved with a
Sense of her Misfortunes (for she was beautiful in her Tears),"
but he could not comfort her. Then the king sent for Eogan,
the murderer of the three sons of Uisneach, "and to torment her
the more made a Present of her to him, to be used at his Pleasure." Eogan placed her in his chariot to drive her to his own
country, and Connor took his place with them for a short way.
The chariot goes forth, and Deirdre, standing between the
king and Eogan, looked at both "with that Sternness and Indig-
nation, that the King took Notice of her, and told her that the
Cast of her eyes between them two, was like the Look of a
Sheep between two Rams." Deirdre was so incensed at this remark that "she started out of the Chariot by Force, and fell
with that Violence upon her Head, that she beat out her Brains,
and instantly died. And this is the Account given by the Records
of Ireland concerning the Death of the unfortunate Deirdre." [90]
Because of the breaking of his safeguard, Fergus MacRoigh
took a bloody revenge on Connor, plundering the palace of

[90] O'Connor, *op. cit.,* pp. 175–81.

Emain Macha and putting all to the sword, "not sparing the Ladies of the Seraglio, whom the King kept for his own Pleasure." [91] Cormac Conloingias also turned against Connor, even though Connor was his father, and he raised an army of about three thousand with which he marched into Connaught and took service under Maeve. Strangely enough, Keating does not tell the story of the great cattle raid of Cooley; the only intimation we get of it is that in the raids Cormac Conloingias conducted by night into Ulster the country of "Crioch Cualigne particularly suffered." [92]

The principal heroes of the Red Branch Keating names as Conal Cearnach, Cuchulin, and Laoghre Buadhach: the greatest is Conal, [93] a reversal of the usually accepted primacy of Cuchulin. [94] Minor stories that he tells of them are numerous; among others are an account of the death of Conchubar as a result of being struck by Meisgeadhra's Ball of Brains, [95] of the killing of Ceat by Conal, [96] of the death of Fergus MacRoigh, [97] and of the death of Maeve. [98] More important than any of these, however, is his version of the tale of Conlaoch, son of Cuchulin. We have seen above a possible variant of this story in the tale of Gorre from the *Book of Howth*. [99]

According to Keating, Cuchulin in his youth had gone to Scotland to study arms of Sgathach, "a lady of masculine Bravery and great Experience." A beautiful young woman of the same country, by name Aoife, conceived

the most violent Passion for him, which she soon found means to acquaint him with. The Cavalier . . . accepted of her Love; . . .

[91] *Ibid.*, p. 179. For a sequel to the Deirdre story, see Whitley Stokes, "The Wooing of Luaine and Death of Athirne," in *Revue Celtique*, 24 (1903), 270–85.

[92] O'Connor, *op. cit.*, p. 179.

[93] *Ibid.*, p. 182.

[94] John A. MacCulloch, *The Mythology of All Races*, III, 139–59.

[95] O'Connor, *op. cit.*, pp. 182–86.

[96] *Ibid.*, p. 188.

[97] *Ibid.*, pp. 190–91.

[98] *Ibid.*, pp. 193–94.

[99] P. 65.

and tho' he had not an Opportunity of marrying her, yet he attempted the Lady's Virtue, who yielded upon the first Summons, and she proved with Child by him.

The hero left Scotland before the child was born; when he went he gave Aoife a chain of gold which the child, if a boy, was to use when he came to man's estate and sought his father. When he saw the chain the father would recognize his son. Cuchulin also left with Aoife three rules the boy should follow in his knight errantry. First, he should never give way to any person living, but should die rather than turn back; second, he should never refuse a challenge but should fight at all hazards; third, he should never confess his name, though he be threatened with death. The boy was taught arms of Sgathach as the father had been, and when he became older he set out to look for his father, steadfastly following the three rules. He arrived at the court of Conchubar but refused his name of the messenger who asked it. In anger, the king sent Cuchulin to deal with the stranger, but still the boy would not tell who he was. At this insolence, the champion became so enraged that he struck the boy with his lance, and in the ensuing fight "the young Hero fell dead upon the Spot by the hands of his own father." [100] This version is followed closely by Lady Gregory in her *Cuchulain of Muir-themne*.[101]

The accounts of Finn and the Fianna that Keating gives do not add a great deal to what we already have. The Fianna were

a standing well disciplined Army under the Monarchs of Ireland (in whose Hands the Militia ever was) that were kept in regular and constant Pay. Their business was to defend the Country against foreign or domestick Enemies, to support the right and succession of their Kings, and to be ready at the shortest Notice upon any Surprise or Emergencies of the State.[102]

[100] O'Connor, *op. cit.*, pp. 196–98.
[101] 4th ed., pp. 313–19.
[102] O'Connor, *op. cit.*, p. 269.

The rules and regulations by which the Fianna lived, as well as the tests a recruit had to pass, are given in full,[103] but tell little that we have not so far learned. Mention is made, however, of the story of Diarmuid and Grania. Grania, Keating says, was one of the daughters of King Cormac, and was married to "Fionn, the Son of Cumhall, but being of an amorous Disposition, she left him and stole away with her Gallant Diarmuid O Duibhne." [104] He dismisses the *Book of Howth's* and Hanmer's theory of the descent of Finn from the Danes; Finn, he maintains, was the son of Cumhall and descended from an ancient king of Leinster.[105]

Keating nowhere mentions in his account of the Fianna the legend of the survival of Oisin until the time of St. Patrick; the nearest he comes to it is in the very beginning of his history when he is discussing the legend of Fiontan, reputed to have lived from before the flood to a time long afterward.[106]

I must own [he says] there is a very good reason for me to believe that there was a very old Man in the time of St. Patrick, who lived some hundred years before; and gave him a particular Account of the History of the Island. . . . The Name of this Person was Tuam the son of Carril, if we believe some Antiquaries, or, if we give credit to others, Roanus, that is, Caoilte Mac Ronain, who was above three hundred years old.[107]

That Keating himself recognized the doubtful truth of many of the stories he tells, he confesses with a disarming air:

If it should be objected, that it is not to be supposed some particular Transactions relating to *O Fionn* and his *Fiana Eirion,* or the *Irish Militia,* can obtain Belief, because some of the Circumstances are impossible in Fact, and therefore must be absolutely False, I confess indeed that the History of *Ireland,* in some degree, labours under the

---

[103] *Ibid.,* pp. 273–75.
[104] *Ibid.,* p. 267.
[105] *Ibid.,* p. 271.
[106] *Ibid.,* pp. 20–21. See James Stephens's "The Story of Tuan MacCairill," *Irish Fairy Tales,* 1923, pp. 1–33.
[107] O'Connor, *op. cit.,* p. 21.

same Misfortune, with most of the old Chronicles that were written in the Times of Idolatry and Paganism; and there is scarce a Country upon Earth, I suppose, whose primitive Records are not disguised with Fable and some incredible Relations; and even since Christianity appeared in the World, and the Clouds of Superstition and Ignorance were, in some Measure, dispell'd, many strange and romantick Accounts have been delivered with an Air of Truth. . . . But it is an unjustifiable Consequence to conclude from hence, that the old Records and Chronicles of all Nations are Fables and Rhapsodies; as if Antiquity were a sure and infallible Mark of Falsehood, and that the antient Writers were a Gang of Cheats and Imposters, who conspir'd together to transmit Lies and to impose upon Posterity.[108]

The man pictures himself in these words: a smiling agnostic, presenting his evidence for us to accept or reject. One suspects strongly that he saw clearly the literary and cultural value of his people's stories of old time and determined to preserve them, caring little about their truth or falsehood.

One thing more of value comes from O'Connor's translation: he translated literally or into blank verse (that sometimes permits of almost literal translation) the Gaelic verses that Keating quotes on almost every page, and therein showed himself wiser than a good many of the eighteenth- and early nineteenth-century translators who made Gaelic poems over into formal English rimed verse. Here is O'Connor's version of the Gaelic poet's picture of St. Columkille doing penance:

> This pious Saint, as a religious Penance,
> Lay on the cold Ground, and thro' his Garments
> His bones looked sharp and meagre; his poor Cell
> Was open to the Inclemency of the Winds,
> Which blew thro' the unplaistered Walls . . .[109]

and of the state of Ireland under Brian Boru—surely an enviable state:

[108] O'Connor, *op. cit.,* p. 268.
[109] *Ibid.,* p. 388.

The Institutes of Bryen Boiroimhe
So wholesome for the support of Virtue,
Were kept with so much Reverence and Regard,
That a young lady of consummate Beauty,
Adorn'd with Jewels and a Ring of Gold;
Travell'd alone on Foot from North to South
And no Attempt was made upon her Honour,
Or to divest her of the Cloaths she wore.[110]

His translation of the lines Keating quotes as having been written about the burial place of the Irish kings and queens near Cruachan were thought good enough by Henry R. Montgomery for reprinting in his *Specimens of the Early Native Poetry of Ireland*.[111] For some strange reason, Montgomery neglects to mention any author; the unwary reader might easily take them for Montgomery's own. A few of the lines of this poem that have about them an air of quiet dignity will bear quoting:

. . . near the mournful Shade
These weeping Marbles cast, are also laid
The great Remains of Conn, who sway'd with Fame
Hibernia's royal Scepter . . .
Nor could thy Beauty, lovely once, secure
Thee, Clothro, or from Death's subduing Arm
Guard thy all-conquering Eyes, whose Lance destroy'd . . .
Thy Sisters Meidbh and Murasg; here entombed
They rest in Silence, near three royal Queens
(Forgetful now in death they ever reign'd)
Eire, Fodhla, Banbha, from the scepter'd Line.[112]

After O'Connor's work no further translations of Keating were published until 1811. In that year the partial translation by William Halliday appeared.[113] In 1866 John O'Mahony did a complete translation that he published in New York; in 1900

---

[110] *Ibid.*, p. 500.
[111] 2nd ed., pp. 86–87.
[112] O'Connor, *op. cit.*, p. 285.
[113] The Introduction and about one-quarter of the text.

Patrick Weston Joyce did Book I, Part I;[114] in 1902–14 David
Comyn and Patrick S. Dineen did a complete translation for the
Irish Texts Society.[115] This last-named is, of course, the most
scholarly and accurate of all the translations; but such a statement cannot detract from the importance of Dermod O'Connor's. Because it was the first and only one published for nearly
a hundred years, his was the one to which the historians and
literary figures of that period perforce turned and the one
through which much knowledge of Irish legend reached the
English-speaking Irish of the eighteenth century.

[114] Dublin.

[115] Vol. I (Vol. 4 of the ITS) by David Comyn, London, 1902; Vols. II
and III (Vols. 8 and 9 of the ITS) by Patrick S. Dineen, London, 1908; Vol.
IV (Vol. 15 of the ITS) by Patrick S. Dineen, London, 1914.

✤ 5 ✤

After Keating

FRANCIS HUTCHINSON's *Defense of the Antient Historians . . . of Ireland and Great Britain* (1734),[116] Walter Harris' translation and edition (1739–64) [117] of the works of Sir James Ware, and Charles O'Conor's *Dissertations on the History of Ireland* (1753) [118] are testimony of the deepening interest in Ireland's past during the mid-eighteenth century. Tantalizingly, Hutchinson in his preface speaks of the Irish natives as having "of late translated many of their old Fragments into English Verse and Prose"; [119] but he prints none of these translations. His book, which is in the form of a dialogue between a Protestant and a Catholic, defends staunchly the work of Walsh, Keating, and MacCurtin; [120] since he himself admits that he knew little Gaelic,[121] his knowledge of Keating very likely came from O'Connor's translation.

Sir James Ware (1594–1666), antiquary and politician who finally rose to the auditor-generalship of Ireland,[122] wrote in Latin; his works dealing with Irish antiquities have, save for his catalogue of the writers of Ireland that is mentioned above,[123] no especial pertinence to this study. Walter Harris, his granddaughter's husband, published besides his translation of Ware

[116] Dublin.
[117] *The Whole Works of Sir James Ware concerning Ireland,* 3 vols., Dublin. An earlier English translation of Ware was published in London in 1705 entitled *The Antiquities and History of Ireland.*
[118] Dublin.
[119] P. v.
[120] See pp. 56–57; 96–97.
[121] Preface, p. xiv: "For altho' I pretend not to understand much of the Language, yet I have several Books written in it, and am no stranger to it's Character and Alphabet."
[122] *DNB.*
[123] P. 46.

a collection of "antient pieces relating to Ireland" called *Hibernica* (1747–50).[124] None of these bear on the myths and legends. Harris, as a matter of fact, finds Irish history defective in its giving way to the foolish telling of fables and myths.[125]

Charles O'Conor (1710–91) was one of the best Irish antiquarians of his day and was one of the first to show up decisively the forgeries of Macpherson, which he does in the second edition (1766) of his *Dissertations*.[126] In the same edition he quotes, without giving the exact source, what he says is Dr. Johnson's opinion on the subject of ancient Irish studies. Far from joining in the current prejudice against the subject or oppressing the writer who undertook it with censure, even where censure was justly due, the doctor said he approved of an effort to revive (as far as they could be usefully revived) the ancient language and literature of a sister isle.[127] But O'Conor's scholarship, unlike Keating's, clouded his appreciation; his book, which is one of comment along with an outline of Irish history, omits reference to anything the author felt to be the least bit fabulous. He even takes Keating severely to task for his telling of the old stories:

Keating's work is a most injudicious Collection; the historical Part is degraded by the fabulous, with which it abounds. Keating was one of those laborious Readers, who, in making Extracts, do it without Selection or Discernment; and such Works . . . ought never to be published.[128]

About 1760 there began a movement in England that came to be known as the "Celtic Revival in English Literature." It lasted until about 1800 and had a marked influence on English literature, especially on the work of Thomas Gray. Its sources were

[124] In two parts, Dublin.

[125] *Hibernica*, p. 136.

[126] *Dissertations on the History of Ireland.* . . . With some remarks on Mr. Macpherson's translation of Fingal and Temora, pp. 22–65.

[127] *Ibid.*, preface, pp. iv–v.

[128] *Ibid.*, p. x.

mostly Welsh and Scotch [129] and were three in number: the
work of Lewis Morris (1702–65), the Welsh antiquarian; the
Works of Ossian (1759–63) of James Macpherson; and *Some
Specimens of the Antient Welsh Bards. Translated into English*
(1764) of Evan Evans. Morris and Evans are of interest only in
that they created some curiosity about Celtic literature as a
whole. Macpherson's influence, of course, was widespread, but
it was felt mainly in England and Europe where it helped force
the growth of the romantic movement. The feeling toward Macpherson in Ireland was mostly one of irritation, for it was felt
that he had dressed Cuchulin and Finn in the kilt and plaid
besides winding the strands of the two great sagas into a Gordian
knot. The steadily growing interest in the matter of Ireland
among the Irish writers followed the paths that the historians and the legitimate translators and scholars were making
slowly.

A number of histories of Ireland appeared during the latter
half of the eighteenth century, and these now claim our attention. The first, Fernando Warner's *History of Ireland,* in two
volumes, was published in London in 1763. Keating is one of
Warner's admitted sources, but the beauty and charm of the
tales told by Keating flee the dusty imagination of Warner.
Of the sorrows of Deirdre and the Tain bo Cooley we read
only that

The original of the quarrel was an Ulster gentleman's stealing a
young lady, whom Connor, to defeat the prophecy of a Druid at her
birth about the disturbances she should occasion, had kept confined
and guarded; and although he had given hostages for their safe return
as a testimony of his pardon, yet he caused the lover and his two
brothers to be assassinated; whose friends, and the hostages themselves resenting this perfidy, took up arms against him, as it has been
said; and retreating into Connaught they interested the Queen and
people of that province in their cause.[130]

[129] See E. D. Snyder, *The Celtic Revival in English Literature 1760–1800.*
[130] I, 206.

Cuchulin is but mentioned as a mighty warrior; the rules and regulations of the Fianna [131] come directly from Keating. Warner's chief value is that Charlotte Brooke used his history as a source for some of the material in her *Reliques of Irish Poetry* (1789).[132]

J. H. Winne's *A Compleat History of Ireland, from the Earliest Accounts to the Present Time,* in two volumes, London, 1774, is worth no more than a cursory glance, for what legend stories Winne tells come from Keating and are much condensed; but Sylvester O'Halloran's *A General History of Ireland from the Earliest Accounts to the Close of the 12th Century* (1778) is of much more than passing interest because it started Standish James O'Grady to work in Irish history, and it was O'Grady's imaginative treatment of the legendary stories in his *History of Ireland* (1878–80) that brought about the interest of Yeats and his fellows in the legends. Ernest Boyd tells us, quoting indirectly from O'Grady himself, that

about the year 1872 a young student [O'Grady] of Dublin University was obliged to spend a wet day indoors at a country house where he was visiting. While exploring the bookshelves he came upon the three volumes of O'Halloran's *History of Ireland,* when he made the interesting discovery that his country had a past.[133]

The author of the history that stirred O'Grady, Sylvester O'Halloran (1728–1807), surgeon and antiquary, was born at Limerick. He studied medicine and surgery at the universities of Paris and Leyden; in 1750 he published *A New Treatise on the Glaucoma, or Cataract,* the first book of its kind to come from the Irish press. He found time, despite a large practice, for literary and antiquarian research; and wrote in 1774 *Ierne De-*

---

[131] I, 249–56.

[132] She quotes, for instance, his description of the rules of the Fianna (*Reliques,* 1789, pp. 40–42); and uses his story of Maon (I, 185–91) as one of her sources for that tale (*Reliques,* 1789, p. 323).

[133] Ernest Boyd, *op. cit.,* p. 27. Boyd is quoting from an article by O'Grady that appeared in the Literary Supplement of *The Irish Homestead* during 1894.

fended, a plea for the validity of ancient Irish history, which was preparation for the work by which he is best known, his *History of Ireland.*[134]

Just what it was about O'Halloran's history that inspired O'Grady is hard to say. The chronological portions are as dull reading as such stuff generally is; the treatment of legend is by no means so full nor so interesting as Keating's. No distinction of any kind is apparent in O'Halloran; O'Grady must have been attracted to his history simply because it was the first account of Ireland he read that told him anything about his native country before the English invasion. Further, since O'Grady's own history is notable especially for its retelling of the heroic tales, the hints of the old stories that he got in O'Halloran undoubtedly inspired him to further research.

O'Halloran's retellings of the legends vary in certain aspects from those we have heretofore noticed; he gives us more of the Tain bo Cooley, for instance, than do any of the other historians. Fergus MacRoy, says O'Halloran, was compelled by Conchubar, the son of Nessa and Fergus's cousin, to flee Ulster. He went to Cruachan, in Connaught, where he was welcomed by Maeve, whose lover he became. She bore him three sons at one birth: a story, as we have seen, told before by MacCurtin. Fergus raised an army

in which some of the most intrepid knights of Ireland went volunteers. In the relation of this famous invasion, yet preserved, called Tani-bho-Cuailgne, or the Spoils of Cattle at Cualgne, in the county of Lowth, we are entertained with the order of the march of the troops. They were led on by Fergus: the queen of Connaught seated in an open chariot, with her Asion, or crown of gold, on her head, followed; her retinue were placed in four chariots more, so disposed, at the sides and rear, that the dust and foam of the cavalry should not stain her royal robes. . . . But though these troops could not force the Ulster army to a general engagement, nor yet gain their end, which was the dethronement of Connor, yet they miserably wasted

[134] *DNB.*

the country, and brought back with them an immense booty, in cattle and other rich effects, notwithstanding the utmost efforts of the Ultonians, though headed by the renowned Conall, and all the champions of Craobh-Ruadh.[135]

A second time Maeve invades Ulster—this time while Conal is away—and Conchubar orders Cuchulin, the second in command, to head the troops but not to join battle until Conal has returned. Cuchulin stays shut up six days, but on the seventh he can no longer contain himself and rushes forth to give battle. But the Ultonians lose the fight and Cuchulin himself is killed; this battle is known as the "Great Defeat at Muir-Theimnhe." [136] So distasteful does O'Halloran find the tales of the magical doings of the druids during this battle, that he mixes censure of them with praise of the old story. "Whilst we admire the style and spirit with which this work is wrote, we are a good deal distressed at the superstition and credulity, which must then have prevailed." [137]

The story of Deirdre is told next, and in so doing O'Halloran shows his unfamiliarity with the logical sequence of the stories in the saga—an unfamiliarity that Keating was not guilty of. Nor does O'Halloran's version agree with Keating's; O'Halloran seems to have heard the outline of the story but not to have bothered about the details. According to him,

The beautiful Deirdre, daughter to Feidhlim, the son of Doill, who was the first minister to the king of Ulster, was educated in the palace of Emania; and amongst the numbers of illustrious youth, companions of the Craobh-Ruadh, who attended the court, were the three sons of Uisneach, whose names were Naois, Ainle, and Ardan. We may judge of the personal accomplishments of the first of them who loved, and was beloved by Deirdre, by the strong terms in which she expressed them. Attended by her confidant on a snowy day, she beheld a butcher at a distance killing a calf, and some time after, a raven come to feed on the blood. The whole woman absorbed in love, turns

---

[135] *A General History of Ireland,* I, 178–79.
[136] *Ibid.,* p. 180.
[137] *Ibid.,* pp. 180–81.

to her governess; "Behold," says she, "the whiteness of that snow,
such is the skin of my hero! his cheeks are more blooming than the
blood scattered round it; and his hair is smoother and blacker than
the feathers of the raven that feeds on it!" Metaphors inexpressibly
bold and strong! After such declaration, we may judge it did not re-
quire much importunity to prevail upon her to elope with her para-
mour.[138]

With one hundred and fifty followers the lovers embarked for
Albany, but Conchubar influenced the Scots' king to force them
to flee; through friends at Conchubar's court they ask forgiveness of him; he "seemed to relent" [139] and sent for them, ap-
pointing as their safeguards his natural son Cormac Conloingios
and his cousin Fergus. (This Fergus is apparently the same one
who O'Halloran told us had long before gone over to Maeve.)
The fugitives return and are slain treacherously soon after their
landing in Ireland by Eogan, Conchubar's man. Then take
place as a result of this treachery renewed wars between Ulster
and Connaught.[140]

In his discussion of Finn, O'Halloran first takes exception to
what he calls Keating's explanation of the name Fine. "Keating and others tell us that these militia were called Fine, from
Fion MacCubhal, but it is certainly a great error; the word Fine,
strictly implying a military corps." [141] The requirements for
getting into the Fianna [142] come from Keating; concerning the
battle of Gabhra in which the Fianna were destroyed, he remarks, with specious reasoning, that

We have yet extant a relation of this battle, supposed to have been
related by Oisin, the father of Osgur, to St. Patrick; but it were absurd
to suppose that he, who was advanced in years at the battle of Gabhra,
should be alive near a century and an half after. . . . Yet as it pre-

[138] Ibid., pp. 181–82.
[139] Ibid., p. 182.
[140] Ibid., pp. 182–83.
[141] Ibid., p. 273.
[142] Ibid., pp. 274–75.

serves the names and actions of the principal heroes on both sides in this most bloody battle, it merits attention.[143]

And so later on, in relating stories of the survival of ancient heroes to the time of St. Patrick, he uses the Oisin tale to prove the truth of Caoilte Mac Ronan's account of the olden days.

The dialogue between St. Patrick and Oisin, still preserved, in which a minute relation is given of the bloody battle of Gabhra, and of the heroes that fell on both sides is another proof of this. The author asserted that he was Oisin, the eldest son of the famous Fion Mac Cumhal; though this battle was fought A.C. 296, at which time Oisin must have been advanced in years.[144]

In itself O'Halloran's work is of no great importance; his history had by no means the widespread influence that O'Connor's Keating had. But the line of descent from Keating to O'Halloran to Standish James O'Grady is direct.

[143] *A General History of Ireland*, I, p. 280.
[144] *Ibid.*, II, 6.

Some Early Translators of Gaelic Poetry

THE last two decades of the eighteenth century are marked by an ever-increasing interest in Gaelic literature and Irish antiquities on the part of the English-speaking Irish. There are a number of landmarks. In 1782 a young man named Charles Henry Wilson published a volume of translations from the Gaelic; in 1785 the Royal Irish Academy was started; in 1786 Joseph Cooper Walker's *Historical Memoirs of the Irish Bards* appeared; in 1789 the retiring and modest Charlotte Brooke finally published her *Reliques of Irish Poetry;* and in 1793 James Hely published his translation of Roderic O'Flaherty's *Ogygia,* written in Latin in 1685. In addition, Theophilus O'Flanagan was doing the preliminary work that was to result in the publication of the *Transactions of the Gaelic Society of Dublin* in 1808. Finally, during these years the redoubtable Charles Vallancey was working with the Gaelic language and Irish antiquities and editing the *Collectanea de Rebus Hibernicis* (1770–1804). Since a consideration of these books and people involves in a number of cases translations of Gaelic poetry into English, and since such translation has not so far loomed very large in our discussion of the matter of Ireland, a rounding up of what references have been made will prove helpful.

These are not many, for only a few writers from the sixteenth to the late eighteenth century did any considerable work in this field. We have noticed [145] that Edmund Spenser had a few translations made for him, as he tells us in his *View of the Present State of Ireland;* that a translation of a Gaelic poem is in the Hanmer papers; [146] that Swift did a semi-translation in "The

[145] P. 68.
[146] Pp. 27–28.

Description of an Irish Feast"; [146a] that O'Connor, in his translation of Keating, did fairly well with the Gaelic poems that Keating quoted; [147] and that Francis Hutchinson, writing in 1734,
spoke of the many translations being made.[147a]

The first translator to be treated here in any detail is Michael
Kearney—whom we have had occasion to consider briefly as one
of the translators of Keating—who in 1635 put into English a
Gaelic poem by John O'Dugan that Kearney titled "The Kings
of the Race of Eibhear." [148] Kearney's quaint introduction de-
serves quotation: "I offer it as I found the same in an ancient
manuscript, deserving you of kindnesse, if by a perfecter Coppie
thereof appearing, yow find any thing hereing misreported, or
misplaced, yow favourably rectifye the mistake or omission by
mee in this behalfe unwillingly committed." [149] Practically nothing is known of Kearney; John Daly, who edited his poem in
1847, speaks of him as a "celebrated scribe . . . of Ballyloskye,
in the County of Crosse Tipperary." [150] Daly attempted to
trace Kearney's history, but the best he could do, he tells us, was
to find that "Ballyloskye . . . lies about three miles below the
town of Nenagh; the ruins of an ancient castle, known as
'Kearney's Castle' stand close to the place, which possibly may
have been his seat." [151]

"The Kings of the Race of Eibhear" is not much of a poem; it
is a dreary recording of the high kings of Ireland from the time
of the Fir-bolgs to the reign of Roderic O'Connor, who ascended
the throne in 1168. Kearney's literal translation is not done with
much imagination, if any; two stanzas—and they are among the
best—will put this point beyond question:

[146a] Pp. 76–77.
[147] Pp. 92–93.
[147a] P. 95.
[148] Edited by John Daly and published in Dublin in 1847 under the title of
The Kings of the Race of Eibhear.
[149] *Ibid.*, p. 7.
[150] *Ibid.*, p. 5.
[151] *Ibid.*

The most important part of pleasant Eire,
Is Munster of the mountain-studded plains,
On account of her nobility, her wealth,
Her store of precious stones, and the honor her people support.
I cannot conceal the good qualities of the men of Munster,
In whom no flaw was ever found;
They were famed for love of freedom, comeliness of countenance,
And loftiness of spirit.[152]

Jonathan Swift's rendering of "Pléaraca na Ruarcach" has been noticed above; [153] in his edition of Swift, Sir Walter Scott prints four lines of this poem as translated by a young man named Charles Henry Wilson—four lines that Swift did not translate—done in the same measure Swift used:

> Here's to you, dear mother.
> I thank you, dear Pat;
> Pitch this down your throat.
> I'm the better of that.[154]

From Scott's note [155] at the beginning of "The Description of an Irish Feast," we have one of the very few references made to Wilson or to his rare book, *Poems Translated from the Irish Language into the English,* that was apparently published in London in 1782. I say "apparently," for I have been unable to get hold of a copy for examination.[156] The book was rare in Scott's day; he speaks of "Mr. Charles Wilson, who published Irish poems in 1782, from whose scarce and forgotten, though very curious collection, I have transferred the original Irish words [of 'Pléaraca na Ruarcach']." [157]

Joseph Cooper Walker also noticed Wilson's translation of this poem in his *Irish Bards:* "A faithful poetical translation of

[152] *Ibid.,* p. 31.
[153] Pp. 76–77.
[154] *Op. cit.,* 2nd ed., XIV, 133.
[155] *Ibid.,* p. 131.
[156] The Union Catalogue of the Library of Congress has no record of it; the British Museum catalogue lists no copy.
[157] *Op. cit.,* 2nd ed., XIV, 131.

Pleraca na Ruarcach has since been published by Charles Wilson, a neglected genius, now struggling with adversity in London." [158] The only other example I know of Wilson's work, besides that quoted by Scott, is in James Hardiman's *Irish Minstrelsy,* where in discussing a poem called "Ode to Drunkenness" Hardiman remarks that

In the year 1792, a translation was published [of the "Ode to Drunkenness" or a book of translations?] by Charles Wilson, a youth of promising genius, who, afterwards repaired to . . . London; where . . . he sunk . . . unnoticed and unknown.[159]

Here are some samplings of the Hardiman quotation; very little about Wilson's ability can be told from his translation of an anonymous Gaelic poet's poem about the lasting and ecstatic joys of liquor:

> At twelve years old I felt thy charms,
> The very name my bosom warms;
> Wed to thy sweets, I cannot rove,
> And age thy beauties will improve.
> Oh! with thee blest beneath the shade,
> In vain dull cares my breast invade;
> . . .
> Deprived of thee, the rich are poor;
> And who is poor of thee possest,
> Thou dearest soother of the breast?
> . . .
> What nymph with thee, say, can compare?
> Thy stream, the ringlet of her hair;
> Thy crystal ray, what eye so bright?
> Transparent azure ting'd with light.[160]

One final reference I found to Wilson's work in Nicholas Kearney's introduction to Volume I of the *Transactions of the Ossianic Society:* "Though Ossianic lore has been almost neg-

[158] *Historical Memoirs of the Irish Bards,* London, 1786, p. 81.
[159] I, 171.
[160] *Ibid.,* p. 172.

lected by most writers, nevertheless it is but fair to record a few honorable and praiseworthy exceptions. The first is C. Wilson, who published a small quarto volume of Ossianic poetry in 1780. . . ." [160a]

Not much more is known of Wilson's life than of his scarce and variously dated volume of translations. According to O'Donoghue's *Poets of Ireland,* he was born at Bailieboro', county Cavan, the son of a rector; studied at Trinity College, Dublin; and subsequently entered the London Middle Temple. For a while he was a Parliamentary reporter. Besides his volume of poems he wrote a few plays, edited a collection of poetry and prose called *Polyantha,* and was the anonymous author of *Brookiana* (2 volumes, London, 1804). He died May 12, 1808. O'Donoghue does not give any basis for his statements, which is unfortunate. [161]

Two translations that I mention simply as additional historical evidence of a growing movement that is to come to a minor climax in the work of Charlotte Brooke and Theophilus O'Flanagan appeared in the *European Magazine, and London Review* for 1782. The first, in the August number, is in prose and is placed in the middle of an anonymous piece entitled "Sentimental Fragments. No. 1." After an account of a dispute between the author and Sophia about the Irish language's possibilities in the gentle art of love, the lady being against and the gentleman for, the latter translates an Irish sonnet to prove his point. Here is the heading of his translation and a few excerpts:

THE SONNET
TRANSLATED FROM THE ORIGINAL IRISH AS NOW SPOKEN IN THE PART OF IRELAND CALLED THE DEASEY'S COUNTRY.

It was on the white hawthorne, on the brow of the valley, I saw the ring of day first break. . . . Rise, my Evalina, soul that informs my heart; do thou smile too, more lovely than the morning in her blushes,

[160a] Dublin, 1854, p. 10.
[161] P. 485.

more modest than the rifled lily, when weeping in her dews . . . the
richness of the wild honey is on thy lips. . . . Black are thy locks . . .
and polished as the raven's smooth pinions.[162]

The second, in the December number, is also a sonnet and was
done by Edward Nolan, Esq., of Dublin. It is headed with the
Irish line "Vurneen deelish vaal ma chree," and two lines of the
translation are enough:

> Thou dear seducer of my heart!
> Fond cause of every struggling sigh! . . .[163]

Of more worth than either of these is a piece in Ritson's *Collection of English Songs* (1783), reprinted from *The Gentleman's Magazine* for October, 1751, entitled "A translation of an
Irish Song beginning Ma ville clane g'un oughth chegh khune,
& c." Ritson claims for this poem "uncommon elegance and
merit"; [164] it is possible to partially endorse his statement:

> Blest were the days, when in the lonely shade,
> Join'd hand in hand my love and I have stray'd,
> Where apple-blossoms scent the fragrant air,
> I've snatch'd soft kisses from the wanton fair.
>
> Then did the feather'd choir in songs rejoice,
> How soft the cuckoo tun'd her soothing voice!
> The gentle thrush with pride display'd his throat,
> Vying in sweetness with the blackbird's note.[165]

The antiquarian labors of Joseph Cooper Walker mark a
definite step forward in the study of Ireland's past. Walker
(1762?–1810) was probably born in Dublin. As a young man,
because of ill health, he went to Italy where he remained for
many years. He busied himself there with studies in Italian
literature and Irish antiquities; the latter subject being one that

---

[162] London, 1782, II, 100.
[163] *Ibid.,* p. 471.
[164] II, 351–52. The "uncommon elegance and merit" is in I, xxxviii.
[165] *The Gentleman's Magazine,* XXI, 467.

increasingly took up his time.[166] Especially was he curious about old Irish music, and after his return to Ireland he published in 1786 *Historical Memoirs of the Irish Bards* [167] which includes, besides a general history of the bards, detailed lives of Cormac Common and Turlough O'Carolan, observations on the music of Ireland, and translations of a number of Gaelic poems.

Walker remarks in his preface that

I trust I am offering to my countrymen an acceptable present: the gift has novelty, at least, to recommend it. Though Ireland has been long famed for its poetry and music, these subjects have never yet been treated of historically. . . . Having taken up my subject at an early period, I was necessitated to explore the dark regions of antiquity. Here a few rays of light darted on me, which only served to make the darkness visible.[168]

Walker's book was sufficiently popular in its day to go into a second edition; [169] its chief value, however, may ultimately prove to lie in the facts that its publication enabled Charlotte Brooke to have printed anonymously in it two of her translations, and that she made use of its material for some of her notes.[170] This follower of Walker's, Miss Charlotte Brooke, is of primary importance in our study. With the possible exception of Dermod O'Connor, the translator of Keating, Charlotte Brooke did more than anyone else until the nineteenth century to make available the matter of Ireland, both in story and song, to the English-speaking Irish.

[166] *DNB.*
[167] London.
[168] *Ibid.,* preface, pp. v–vi.
[169] Dublin, 1818, 2 vols.
[170] See below, p. 111; and the *Reliques,* pp. 91–92; 234–36; 240–45; 260–61; etc.

ᵹ 7 ᵹ

Charlotte Brooke

CHARLOTTE BROOKE was born at Rantavan, county Cavan, in 1740.[171] She was the daughter of Henry Brooke (1703–83) who was the author of, among numerous other works, that surprisingly well-told moral tale, *The Fool of Quality* (1760–62), and *Gustavus Vasa* (1739), a tragedy. She has been called "the well-beloved and flattering child of his old age." [172] She was educated by her father in literature, music, and art; "such were his talents of instruction, and her facility of retaining it, that in her fifth year she was able to read, distinctly and rapidly, any English book." [173] Another side of her father's instruction comes to us most clearly perhaps from the anecdote of him that tells how the congregation of the church Mr. Brooke attended asked him one Sunday morning, in the absence of the minister, to take the pulpit.

He consented, and the prayers being over with he opened the Bible and preached extempore on the first text that struck his eye. In the middle of his discourse the clergyman entered and found the whole congregation in tears. He entreated Mr. Brooke to proceed; but this he modestly refused; and the other as modestly declared, that, after the testimony of superior abilities, which he perceived *in the eyes of all present,* he would think it presumptive and folly to hazard anything his own.[174]

Charlotte's interest in the Gaelic language was first aroused when she heard one of her father's laborers read to an im-

171 Desmond Ryan, *The Sword of Light,* p. 43. Ryan does not give the source for his statement; he admits (p. 43) that he is one of the few biographers of Charlotte willing to name her birth date.

172 Aaron Crossly Seymour, "A Memoir of Her Life and Writings," prefixed to the *Reliques,* 2nd ed., Dublin, 1816, p. 8.

173 *Ibid.*

174 Richard Ryan, *Biographia Hibernica,* p. 210.

promptu audience in the fields stories of Oisin and Cuchulin from a collection of manuscripts in Gaelic that he owned.[175] And her father must have urged her on in the study of Gaelic and things Irish, for he himself was deeply interested in the Gaelic language and Irish antiquities; at one time he proposed to write a history of Ireland.[176] Joseph Cooper Walker, who was a close friend of the Brooke family for many years, likewise encouraged Charlotte in her Gaelic studies and persuaded her to let him print in his *Irish Bards* her translations of a song and monody by Carolan.[177] In characteristic fashion she steadfastly refused to permit her name to be printed as the author.

Spurred on, therefore, by her father and Walker, as well as by her own inclinations, she commenced work in 1787 on the *Reliques of Irish Poetry* that she published in Dublin in 1789. In 1791 appeared her *The School for Christians, in Dialogues, for the use of Children;* and later in the same year an edition of her father's works with a memoir. From none of these publications, however, did she make much money; her last years were spent in poverty in a small cottage near Longford, where she died on March 29, 1793.[178] Something of her character, as seen by her contemporaries, can be gleaned from the following lines, said to have been attached to a portrait of her:

> Religious, fair, soft, innocent, and gay,
> As evening mild, bright with the morning ray,
> Youthful and wise, in ev'ry grace mature,
> What vestal ever led a life so pure.
> By W. W-M-N.[179]

The work of hers that particularly concerns us here is, of course, the *Reliques of Irish Poetry: consisting of Heroic Poems,*

---

[175] Desmond Ryan, *op. cit.,* pp. 41–42.

[176] Snyder, *op. cit.,* pp. 114–17.

[177] "Carolan's Monody on the Death of Mary MacGuire" (*Irish Bards,* Dublin, 1818, I, 321–23); and "Tiagharna Mhaighe-eo" (*Irish Bards,* I, 336–39).

[178] *Anthologia Hibernica,* I (April 1793), 324.

[179] Aaron Seymour, *op. cit.,* p. 103.

*Odes, Elegies, and Songs, translated into English verse: with
Notes Explanatory and Historical; and the Originals in the Irish
Character. To Which is Subjoined an Irish Tale.* With the exception of Wilson's volume, noted above, the *Reliques* is the first
book by an Irish writer that is devoted entirely to the translation
of genuine (shown by her printing of the original Gaelic poems)
Gaelic poetry into English; and, unlike Wilson's book [180] that
apparently passed almost unnoticed, was received with acclaim
and was circulated widely not only in Ireland but also in England. Before considering the poems themselves, let us look at
certain of the passages in Miss Brooke's preface for the indica-
tion they give of the purpose and plan of her work.

With a view [she says] to throw some light on the antiquities of this
country, to vindicate, in part, its history, and prove its claim to scientific as well as to military fame, I have been induced to undertake
the following work. Besides the four different species of composition
which it contains, (the Heroic Poem, the Ode, the Elegy, and the
Song) others yet remain inattempted by translation:—the Romance,
in particular, which unites the fire of Homer with the enchanting
wildness of Ariosto. But the limits of my present plan have necessarily excluded many beautiful productions of genius, as little more
can be done, within the compass of a single volume, than merely to
give a few specimens, in the hope of awakening a just and useful curiosity, on the subject of our poetical compositions. . . . I do not pro-
fess to give merely a literal version of my originals, for that I should
have found an impossible undertaking . . . there are many complex
words that could not be translated literally. . . . It is really astonish-
ing of what various and comprehensive powers this neglected language is possessed. In the pathetic it breathes the most beautiful and
affecting simplicity; and in the bolder species of composition, it is
distinguished by a force of expression, a sublime dignity, and rapid
energy, which it is scarcely possible for any translation fully to con-
vey; as it sometimes fills the mind with ideas altogether new, and
which, perhaps, no modern language is entirely prepared to express. [181]

[180] See above, pp. 105–7.
[181] *Reliques,* Dublin, 1789, pp. v–vi. Note the similarity between the latter

These comments on the difficulty of translating Gaelic into English are interesting, I think, in view of the new rhythms and new arrangements of sentence structure that Sir Samuel Ferguson, Douglas Hyde, John Millington Synge, and others were to use years later in trying to express the idiom of Gaelic in English.

The British Muse [she remarks later] is not yet informed that she has an elder sister in this isle; let us then introduce them to each other! together let them walk abroad from their bowers, sweet ambassadresses of cordial union between two countries that seem formed by nature to be joined by every bond of interest, and of amity. . . . Let them come—but will they answer to a voice like mine? [182]

(One might reply, in answer to Miss Brooke's question, that while probably the two Muses will not rush in their coming they will at least look at each other.)

The material matter of Miss Brooke's poems and the translations themselves must be gone into. The heroic poems are chiefly from the Red Branch and the Finn cycles; the opening poem, "Conloch," is the story of Cuchulin's killing his son.[183] Miss Brooke translated from an original Gaelic manuscript in her possession; the poem is prefaced with a discourse by Sylvester O'Halloran,[184] the historian, in which he tells in prose the story of Conloch. This account is mostly the same as Keating's, save that Cuchulin, rather than learning arms in Scotland at the time of his affair, is simply passing through that country on his way home from a continental expedition. He meets and falls in love with Aoife; and, in O'Halloran's own phrase of unconscious humor, "the affairs of his country calling him home, he left the lady pregnant." [185] The translation itself is in the form of an ode, the measure varying from trimeter to

---

part of this quotation and the letter quoted by Snyder, *op. cit.,* pp. 71–72, written to the *Scots Magazine,* January 1756.

[182] *Ibid.,* pp. vi–vii.
[183] See above, pp. 65–66.
[184] Brooke, *op. cit.,* pp. 3–8.
[185] *Ibid.,* p. 7.

pentameter; the verses are rhymed. Not the slightest originality of structure or diction is shown.

In the course of "Conloch," Miss Brooke takes occasion, when Cuchulin mentions "ye fav'rite sons of fame" [186]—meaning the sons of Usnach—to tell in a footnote the story of Deirdre.[187] In a number of points this version differs from the others we have considered: Deirdre is shut up and guarded simply to "frustrate the policy of a Druid, who had foretold at her birth, that she should be fatal to the house of Ulster." [188] When Deirdre entreats a sight of Naisi, Lavarcham goes to him and "extolled her pupil's charms, and promised to indulge him with an interview, provided he would, on his part, engage to free the fair captive, and make her his wife." [189] Miss Brooke does not give the source for her variant.

Following "Conloch" is "The Lamentation of Cucullin, over the Body of his son Conloch." Two specimens of this translation, that is also in the form of an ode, will show some of Miss Brooke's feeling for poetry. In the first, the champions of the Red Branch have all, with the exception of Cuchulin, been overcome by the presumptuous Conloch; a messenger is sent for the mighty chief:

> Quick let a rapid courier fly!
> (Indignant Auliffe cried,)
> Quick with the shameful tidings let him hie,
> And to our aid the first of heroes call,
> From fair Dundalgan's lofty wall,
>   Or Dethin's ancient pride.[190]

In the second, Cuchulin, though mourning his own son, sorrows likewise for the three sons of Usnach. (The Conloch episode happened, therefore, after the death of Deirdre.)

[186] Brooke, *op. cit.*, p. 13.
[187] *Ibid.*, note i, pp. 13–16.
[188] *Ibid.*, note i, p. 13.
[189] *Ibid.*
[190] *Ibid.*, p. 12.

Lo, the sad remnant of my slaughter'd race,
Like some lone trunk, I wither in my place!—
No more the sons of Usnoth to my sight
Give manly charms, and to my soul delight!
No more my Conloch shall I hope to see;
Nor son, nor kinsman now survives for me!
O my lost son!—my precious child, adieu!
No more these eyes that lovely form shall view!
No more his dark-red spear shall Ainle wield!
No more shall Naoise thunder o'er the field!
No more shall Ardan sweep the hostile plains!—
Lost are they all, and nought but woe remains!—
Now, chearless earth, adieu thy every care:
Adieu to all, but Horror and Despair! [191]

The curious mingling of regret for Conloch and the three sons of Usnach in this extract suggests that in some versions the two tragic stories almost became one; in this case one can easily imagine the substitution of Deirdre for Conloch.

Three Oisinic poems—"Magnus the Great," "The Chase," and "Moira Borb"—are next; they retell, in the familiar framework of dialogue between Oisin and St. Patrick, stories of the Finn cycle. The tale of the first, "Magnus," is of no great moment; it concerns simply a battle between the Fenians and a hostile army. But the dialogue in the poem between the two great champions of the heathen and Christian worlds shows the old pagan stormily defying Patrick and his religion. Oisin's opening remarks, for instance, are full of bitterness:

> I care not for thee, senseless clerk!
> Nor all thy psalming throng,
> Whose stupid souls, unwisely dark,
> Reject the light of song . . . [192]

A hundred years later Yeats has Oisin say:

> Patrick, before thy craft dies each old song. [192a]

[191] *Ibid.,* pp. 30–31.
[192] *Ibid.,* p. 37.
[192a] W. B. Yeats, *The Wanderings of Oisin and other Poems*, London. 1889, p. 30.

Miss Brooke introduces into the dialogue what is almost bully-ing when Oisin brutally wants to know why he has let Patrick live so long:

> Why did my folly let thee live,
> To brave too patient age,
> To see how tamely I forgive,
> And preach me from my rage!

And Patrick humbly apologizes:

> Pardon, great chief!—I meant no ill;
> Sweet is to me thy song;
> And high the themes and lofty skill
> Its noble strains prolong.[193]

At the poem's end, Oisin contrasts his happy former days with his present state:

> Now old,—the streams of life congeal'd,
> Bereft of all my joys!
> No sword this wither'd hand can wield,
> No spear my arm employs.[194]

The same strain is found in the close of Yeats's poem, when the old warrior laments:

Ah me! to be old without succor, a show unto children, a stain,
Without laughter, a coughing, alone with remembrance and
     fear . . .[195]

In her notes to "Magnus the Great," Miss Brooke tells of the rules and regulations of the Fianna, which she copied from Warner's *History of Ireland*.[196]

The second of the Oisinic poems, "The Chase," is the story of an enchantment of Finn and how the enchantment was finally broken and Finn restored. Again, the poem is of little

[193] Brooke, *op. cit.,* p. 38.
[194] *Ibid.,* p. 65.
[195] Yeats, *op. cit.,* p. 52.
[196] Brooke, *op. cit.,* note d, pp. 39-42.

worth; and, again, we like best the dialogue between Oisin and Patrick. Now it is milder; each is willing to grant the other some good qualities. Yet Oisin hurls two lines of abuse that deserve quoting:

> Now, Patrick of the scanty store,
> And meager-making face! [197]

"Moira Borb," the last of the Finn poems, relates how a maiden came to Finn and asked his protection from her pursuer; it is granted, and in the ensuing fight, though many Fenians are killed, the girl is saved.[198]

The songs and elegies of the Gaelic bards of historic times that Miss Brooke translates have in them her best poetry. Rarely, for instance, does she excel these lines; and rarely equal them:

> Then once more, at early morn,
> Hand in hand we should be straying,
> Where the dew-drop decks the thorn,
> With its pearls the woods arraying.[199]
>
> . . .
>
> Sweet would seem the holly's shade,
> Bright the clust'ring berries glowing,
> And, in scented bloom array'd,
> Apple-blossoms round us blowing.[200]

The Irish tale prefixed to *The Reliques* is called "Mäon," [201] and is the story of Cobthach, who ascends the throne of Ireland through murder, but is himself brought to grief by the brave Mäon, son of one of his victims. The source of this story is in Keating and Warner; [202] interestingly enough, the same

[197] *Ibid.*, p. 115.
[198] *Ibid.*, pp. 121–34.
[199] *Ibid.*, p. 209.
[200] *Ibid.*, p. 210.
[201] *Ibid.*, pp. 321–69.
[202] O'Connor's Keating, London, 1723, pp. 158–61; Warner, *op. cit.*, I, 185–91.

legend was recently told by Padraic Colum in *The Story of Lowry Maen*.[203]

Miss Brooke gives in her notes a number of prose translations;[204] these as a rule are far superior to the conventional and rather stilted verse into which she customarily translates. Her prose rendering of Carolan's "Song for Gracey Nugent," for example, is a not too unworthy predecessor of Douglas Hyde's translations in the *Love Songs of Connacht*:[205]

I will sing with rapture of the Blossom of Whiteness!
Gracey, the young and beautiful woman, who bore away the palm of excellence in sweet manners and accomplishments, from all the Fair-ones of the provinces . . .
Her side like alabaster and her neck like the swan, and her countenance like the Sun in summer. How blest is it for him who is promised, as riches, to be united to her, the branch of fair curling tendrils . . .
I say to the Maid of youthful mildness that her voice and her converse are sweeter than the songs of the birds!
There is no delight or charm that imagination can conceive but what is found ever attendant on Gracey.[206]

The *Reliques* is a scholarly book; for each poem the sources of the story the poem tells are given, and wherever possible something of the history of the manuscript with which the translator worked. Mostly the sources are to be found in the histories of Keating, Warner, and O'Halloran; but Miss Brooke was familiar also with Stanihurst,[207] Cambrensis,[208] Spenser,[209] and Hanmer.[210] In one case she quotes from the *Book of Howth* that "they [the Fianna] were *all* destroyed, Oisin excepted; and that he lived till the arrival of St Patrick, to whom he related

[203] New York, 1937.
[204] Pp. 89–90, 94, 134, etc.
[205] Dublin, 1894.
[206] Brooke, *op. cit.*, p. 247.
[207] *Ibid.*, note f, p. 57.
[208] *Ibid.*, note e, p. 57.
[209] *Ibid.*, note, p. 55.
[210] *Ibid.*, note g, p. 82.

the exploits of the Fenii." [211] Here is additional proof—if more were needed—that the legends as told by the early historians and chroniclers discussed above were used by the poets of a later time.

For a work of its kind, the criticism that the *Reliques,* as well as its author, attracted was widespread and very favorable; nor was this criticism, as we shall show, contemporary only. The *Critical Review* for July 1790, after a twelve-page discussion, says:

To the poetical talents of her Gaelic ancestors and her own, we pay respect. We have been entertained with her translations from every different species of composition mentioned in the title page, and recommend her performance to the antiquary and man of genius.[212]

A favorable nine-page notice in the *Monthly Review* for 1791 speaks of Miss Brooke as being "so perfectly in possession of the language of poetry, that her . . . whole work is interesting to English readers." [213]

When she died in 1793, the *Anthologia Hibernica* for April of that year eulogized her as "the celebrated and accomplished Miss Charlotte Brooke"; [214] in the same issue a poem "To the memory of Miss Charlotte Brooke" appeared.[215] Crofton Croker, in his *Researches in the South of Ireland,* says of the *Reliques* that "this work will continue to hold an eminent place when the productions of those who condescend to patronize the writer are forgotten"; [216] Richard Ryan, in the *Biographia Hibernica,* speaks of it as "a work universally admired . . . affording gratification both to the antiquary and lover of poetry." [217] And the *Dublin Penny Journal* for September 1, 832, in an article entitled "Miss Brooke," becomes rhapsodic:

[211] *Ibid.,* note g, p. 147.
[212] LXX (July–December 1790), 34. The whole review is on pages 22–34.
[213] Series 2, IV (January–April 1791), 46. The whole review is on pp. 37–46.
[214] I, 324.
[215] I, 307.
[216] P. 333.
[217] P. 211.

"There are few writers, male or female, to whom we think
Ireland owes a greater debt of gratitude than to Miss Charlotte
Brooke, a lady whose patriotism led her to translate some of
our most beautiful poetical remains, and whose talent enabled
her to do them ample justice." [218]

Appreciation of her continued down through the nineteenth
century.[219] In 1853 Nicholas Kearney mentions her as one of
the "few honorable and praiseworthy exceptions" [219a] who had
before Kearney's day treated Ossianic lore; in 1879, Patrick
Weston Joyce, in the preface to his *Old Celtic Romances,*
speaks of "the true interpretation of the spirit of these old romances, prose and poetry," that had been caught by Charlotte
Brooke; [220] in 1899, Douglas Hyde, in *A Literary History of
Ireland,* gives her credit for being the first to use the word
"Fenian." [221] In this, however, Hyde is wrong; the honor apparently belongs to Charles Vallancey, who in 1786 in an essay
on the Gaelic language uses the phrase "The dialect of the
Fenians, the tongue of the Fenians." [222] Her latest admirer is
Desmond Ryan, who in *The Sword of Light* devotes a chapter

[218] I, 74–75.

[219] See, for instance, Thomas M'Louchlan, *The Dean of Lismore's Book,*
pp. lviii, lxxvii, 22, *n.;* and Henry R. Montgomery, *op. cit.,* new edition, pp. 6,
33–43, 67–80, 140–50, 211–14, 249–55, 279–82.

[219a] *Op. cit.,* p. 10.

[220] 2nd ed., London, 1894, p. vii, *n.*

[221] P. 364, *n.:* "The first person who appears to have used it is Miss Brooke,
as early as 1796: in her translation of some Ossianic pieces, I find the lines—
He cursed in rage the Fenian chief
And all the Fenian race."
Hyde is mixed in his dates, for Miss Brooke died in 1793. Furthermore, the
lines he quotes (from "The Chase," *Reliques,* 1789, p. 106) are misquoted.
They should read:
He cursed with rage the Finian chief,
And all the Finian race.
Hyde makes two other references to Miss Brooke: one (*Literary History,* p. 301,
n.) to her "Lamentation of Cuchulin"; the other (*Lit. His.,* p. 361, *n.* 4) to her
"Conloch."

[222] *Collectanea de Rebus Hibernicis,* II, 62.

to her and her father.[223] There seems to be little doubt that as the forces which led to the literary revival of the late nineteenth century are better understood, her importance will increase.

[223] Pp. 40–58. See also my article, "Charlotte Brooke: A Forerunner of the Celtic Renaissance," in *The General Magazine and Historical Chronicle* of the University of Pennsylvania, XL (January 1938), 2, 178–83.

To the Nineteenth Century

WE come back briefly, and for the last time, to the historians with a consideration of James Hely's English translation of Roderick O'Flaherty's *Ogygia, or a Chronological Account of Irish Events,* written originally in Latin in 1685, and published in Dublin in 1793. Not a great deal of legendary material is in the *Ogygia.* Concerning the Red Branch cycle, O'Flaherty says that Fergus MacRoy, dethroned by Conchubar in the third year of his reign, took refuge in Connaught where he enlisted under the banner of Maeve. From her Fergus got assistance for an attack on Ulster; the hostilities lasted seven years,

which hostile preparations have been blazoned and embellished by the poetical fictions of those ages. About the middle of this war, eight years prior to the Christian aera, Mauda queen of Connaught in conjunction with Fergus Rogy, carried off an immense quantity of cattle, memorable for the egregious valour of those who drove and pursued them from Cualgny in the County of Louth.[224]

A chapter is devoted to Cuchulin and Conal Cearnach: Cuchulin was but seventeen years old when he pursued the "Cualgnian plunder"; [225] Cuchulin's father and Conal were the first men in Ireland to break horses to the saddle.[226] The only notice O'Flaherty makes of Deirdre is in his recitation of Cuchulin's lineage, and peculiarly enough, she is incidental to the mention of Naisi:

Cuculand, by his mother, was related to the kings of Ulster . . . from whom he was descended. Dechtira was his mother; Cathbad, the druid, was his grandfather; his grandmother, by his mother, was

---

[224] *Ogygia,* London, 1793, II, 154.
[225] *Ibid.,* p. 161.
[226] *Ibid.,* p. 162.

Nessa, the daughter of Achy Sulbhuidhe; his uncles were Conquover Nessan, king of Ulster, and Cormac his son; his aunts were Inlenda, and Finncoema, the mother of Conall Kearnach. Inlenda, the daughter of Cathbad, had three sons by her uncle Ustenn, the son of Congal, king of Ireland; 1. Nis, the husband of Derdria, son-in-law to Fedlim Dall, chamberlain to Conquovar Nessan, king of Ulster; 2. Annly, son-in-law to Eugenius, son to Durthact, lord of Fernmoy; and 3. Ardann.[227]

Cuchulin dies when he is twenty-seven years old by the "swords of the sons of Calitin; or, as Tigernach writes, was assassinated by Lugad, grandson of Carbry Niafear, king of Leinster." [228]

Even less is told of Finn and the Fianna than of the Red Branch heroes. Finn was Cormac MacArt's son-in-law, "married to his daughter Grania, but as she eloped with Diermoit O'Duibhne he had his other daughter Albea married to him." [229] Finn was

generalissimo of the Irish militia, highly distinguished for his jurisprudence, dissertations on which written by him are extant; for his poetical compositions in his native language, and as some write, for his prophecies, he has, on account of his noble military exploits, afforded a vast field of panegyric and encomium to the poets, he was reconciled to his wife, after she had by an illicit connection with Diermot, Donnchad, Illand, Ruchlad, and Herod.[230]

The battle of Gabhra occurs after the death of Finn.[231]

Amusing proof that O'Flaherty could not distinguish between fact and myth is shown by his discussion of Manannan:

The merchant, Orbsen [son of Allad, of the Tuatha De Danann, according to O'Flaherty], was remarkable for carrying on a commercial intercourse between Ireland and Britain: he was commonly called Manannan Mac Lir, that is Manannan, on account of his intercourse with the isle of Mann; and Mac Lir, i.e. *Sprung of the Sea,* because

[227] *Ibid.*
[228] *Ibid.*
[229] *Ibid.*, p. 242.
[230] *Ibid.*
[231] *Ibid.*

he was an expert diver;—besides, he understood the dangerous parts
of harbours; and, from his prescience of the change of weather, always avoided tempests.[232]

The only review of Hely's work I have found was in the
Anthologia Hibernica for March 1793; it said that Hely did a
fairly good job, but that O'Flaherty's work was based on the
"fleeting and unsubstantial tales of Bards and Seanachies." [233]
From our point of view this is not a criticism; we think it unfortunate that O'Flaherty did not tell more of these "fleeting
and unsubstantial tales." If he had had the ability of a Keating he might have done so; nevertheless, the *Ogygia,* because
of the condensed form of its legends and their variations from
what we have so far had, has some value in our study.

The work of General Charles Vallancey (1721–1812) has
been given, it seems to me, a prominence out of all propor-
tion to its value.[234] This army engineer, who came to Ireland
in 1762 to make a military survey and became interested in
Ireland's antiquities,[235] was the editor of the *Collectanea de
Rebus Hibernicis* (1770–1804), that reached ultimately six volumes. Burrowes, in the preface to the first volume of the *Transactions of the Royal Irish Academy* (1787), says that the
Collectanea came about in the following manner:

In the year 1772 the antient state of Ireland attracted the attention of
the Dublin Society, who appointed a committee for the express purpose of enquiring into its antiquities. . . . The meetings of the . . .
committee after about two years ceased, but the zeal of a very few of
their members still continuing has given to the public several essays,
since comprised . . . [in the] . . . *Collectanea de Rebus Hibernicis.*[236]

---

[232] *Ogygia,* London, 1793, II, 154, p. 26.

[233] *Ibid.,* I, 202.

[234] It is a little difficult to see why his work should be so fully listed by the
Cambridge Bibliography, New York, 1941, III, 1047–48, and Meredith Hanmer,
for just one example, not even mentioned.

[235] *DNB.*

[236] Dublin, I, xiv.

Vallancey was the author also of an *Essay on the Celtic Language* that he published in 1772, and he included in the same volume a grammar of the language. His attempts to collate that language with the Algonkin of North America, the Oscan, the Showiah of Africa, and the Shilhae of Africa are the wild speculations of a man with but a smattering of linguistics.

Vallancey was one of the principal contributors to the *Collectanea*,[237] but the value of that collection lies not in Vallancey's contributions but in the essays done for it by men like Joseph Cooper Walker and Charles O'Conor. The best we can say for Vallancey is that he stimulated interest in Irish antiquities without producing anything of real value himself; and also that he may have encouraged and helped Theophilus O'Flanagan in the prosecution of O'Flanagan's work, for the two men were close friends.

But Theophilus O'Flanagan (1762–1814), a consideration of whose work will carry us over into the nineteenth century and will end this part of our study, while perhaps thankful for encouragement probably needed very little help in his antiquarian researches, for from all indications he was a scholar of quite different stamp from Vallancey. He was born near Tulla, county Clare, and attended Trinity College, Dublin, where he received his B.A. in 1789. From his graduation to his death he followed the profession of teaching, and cultivated constantly an innate fondness for whiskey which lost him several positions. His ability as a scholar, especially as a linguist familiar with Gaelic, brought him to prominence among the Irish intellectuals of the day.[238] He himself was so sure of his ability that he made the surprising statement that there were not "in the whole nation three men conversant in the Irish language." [239] Both Walker and Hely pay him tributes; [240]

[237] The contents are on pp. 2749–50 of Lowndes *Bibliographer's Manual*, Bohn's ed., London, 1857–64, Vol. V, pt. 2.
[238] *DNB*.
[239] P. 47, *n.*, in his translation of Lynch's *Cambrensis Eversus*.
[240] Walker, *Irish Bards*, preface, i, "Had I not been favored with the aid

from mention of him time and again by Charlotte Brooke [241]
he was evidently of much help to her in the writing of the
Reliques.

The great labor of O'Flanagan's life was his editing of the
first and only volume of *Transactions of the Gaelic Society of
Dublin* (1808). This society, founded in 1806 "for the investigation and revival of Ancient Irish Literature," [242] numbered
among its members Joseph Cooper Walker, Sylvester O'Halloran, Charles Vallancey, and, above all, Theophilus O'Flanagan, the secretary and moving spirit. Their program was an
ambitious one. Concerning the Gaelic language, their ad-
vertisement speaks of it as "the language of Japhet, spoken
before the Deluge, and probably the language of Paradise." [243]
Such claim is made on the authority of Shaw's *A Gaelic and
English Dictionary* (1780). [244] The Society planned the publication of "every Fragment existing in the Gaelic Language,
the History of Ireland, by Dr. Keating," adding that "the original Gaelic with a new translation will shortly be put to
press." [245] (The partial translation by William Halliday in 1811
was sponsored by the Society.)

---

of Mr. Theophilus O'Flanagan of Trinity College, Dublin, I should often had
reason to regret, in the prosecution of my enquiries, that my knowledge of the
Irish language is so very confined"; Hely, *op. cit.*, preface, I, xi, "I must confess, (and I am proud I can do it with heartfelt gratitude) that I stand highly
indebted to Theophilus O'Flanagan, Esq., of Trinity College, for his attention
and friendship, in the prosecution of this work. His profound knowledge of
the language and antiquities of this country, has enabled me to present it
more perfect and intelligible to all descriptions of my countrymen, than I
otherwise possibly could."

[241] She thanks him (the *Reliques,* p. 179) for the original of an "Ode," by
Fitzgerald; again (p. 189) for the original of "Elegy to the Daughter of
Owen"; and (p. 199) for the original of an "Elegy" that O'Flanagan took
down from the dictation of a young Mayo woman.

[242] Title page.

[243] *Ibid.*, preface, p. vii.

[244] Preface, p. 6.

[245] *Transactions of the Gaelic Society,* preface, p. vii.

There are still in existence a variety of tracts in history, Genealogy, Law, Physics, Poetry, and Romance. . . . An opportunity is now, at length, offered to the Learned in Ireland to retrieve their character among the nations of Europe, and shew that their History and Antiquities are not fitted to be consigned to eternal oblivion; the Plan, if pursued with spirit and perseverance, will redound much to the Honor of Ireland.[246]

The *Transactions* contains an essay on the Gaelic language by P. M'Elligott;[247] an English verse and Latin prose translation of a Gaelic poem, "Advice to a Prince" (by Thaddy Mac-Brady, a Gaelic poet), by O'Flanagan;[248] a literal translation, from a manuscript in his possession, of the Deirdre story by O'Flanagan, followed by an "historical" version of the same story (from Keating?) also by O'Flanagan;[249] a literal translation of a Gaelic poem "Colum Kill's Farewell to Aran" by O'Flanagan;[250] a verse translation of "The Blackbird of the Grove of Carna" (an Oisinic poem) by William Leahy;[251] a verse translation of "The Tale of Talc" (an Oisinic poem) also by Leahy;[252] and a literal translation of "The Marks of Finn MacComhal's Greyhound" by O'Flanagan.[253] Of primary importance among these is O'Flanagan's literal translation of that part of the Deirdre story as told in the Gaelic manuscript he owned; it is not too much to say that with this addition to what we already have the tale of Deirdre in English reaches full growth.

The full title O'Flanagan uses is *Deirdre, or, The Lamentable Fate of the Sons of Usnach, An Ancient Dramatic Tale, One*

[246] *Ibid.*, preface, pp. vii–viii.
[247] "Observations on the Gaelic Language," pp. 1–40. The paging of the *Transactions* starts anew in several places.
[248] *Ibid.*, pp. 1–54.
[249] *Ibid.*, pp. 1–178.
[250] *Ibid.*, pp. 179–89.
[251] *Ibid.*, pp. 196–98.
[252] *Ibid.*, pp. 205–11.
[253] *Ibid.*, p. 215.

of the three tragic stories of Erin; Literally translated into English, from an original Gaelic Manuscript, With Notes and observations. To which is annexed, The old historic account of the facts on which the story is founded. In the proem he acknowledges help from Keating and incidentally pays the great historian tribute: "All the copies [of the Deirdre story] are defective in not giving the birth and education of Deirdre. . . . This I am induced to supply from the learned Dr. Keating, who tells every story well." [254] Then follows the beginning of the Deirdre story as told by Keating—differing in no essential, it should be noted, from the gist of O'Connor's translation of Keating—to the point where Fergus and Cormac Conloingas leave Conchubar to fetch Deirdre and the sons of Usnach from their exile.[255] The remainder of the tale O'Flanagan gives us from his "original Gaelic manuscript."

Conchubar, in the midst of a feast he is holding for his nobles, asks them if anything is wanting; they answer "No." But Conchubar disagrees; he says the sons of Usnach are wanting. The nobles, delighted at what seems forgiveness on the King's part, shout assent. Thereupon the King remarks that Naisi had agreed to come back only under the safeguard of Conal Cearnach, Cuchulin, or Fergus MacRoy; and he calls each of these apart in turn and asks him what he would do if his safeguard were violated. Conal and Cuchulin reply they would kill any man, even the King, who did so; Fergus replies he would kill any but the King. So the King chooses Fergus as his messenger to Naisi; and Fergus goes for the lovers, accompanied by Illan and Buini, his two sons. When they return to Ireland with the lovers, they are met on their landing by Barach, a close friend of Conchubar's, who puts obligations on Fergus to attend a feast at his castle. Although dismayed, Fergus knows he must honor his bonds of knighthood and go with Barach; he sends Illan and Buini on to the capital with Deirdre

[254] "Deirdri," p. 1.
[255] *Ibid.*, pp. 1-9.

and the sons of Usnach as guarantee of their safekeeping.

Deirdre is filled with unquiet; and when she and the brothers and the sons of Fergus are lodged for the night in the Red Branch House instead of in the royal palace, her unquiet becomes a great fear of the mind of the King.

While the King is supping moodily alone, he remembers the beauty of Deirdre and is troubled. He tells Lavarcam, Deirdre's old nurse, to fetch word of it. The nurse hastens and warns the lovers of the growing treachery in the King's heart; she says to close well the doors and windows of the Red Branch House. To the King, Lavarcam laughs that Deirdre has beauty no longer, and he is contented. But in a little space her old beauty comes to him again, and now he must ask Trendon to seek her out and bring word if loveliness is still on her. Trendon spies one open window in the Red Branch House; he peers within and gloats at Deirdre and Naisi playing chess. But Deirdre, nervous and watchful, sees him and calls to Naisi who throws a chessman at Trendon and knocks his eye out. When Trendon tells the King his story and how the beauty of Deirdre is unchanged, the King says, "The man of that throw would be king of the world if he have not short life." [256]

Now by the King's orders his troops surround the Red Branch House and call for surrender; they are answered with scorn. The besieged make sorties against them; the first to go out is Buini, the son of Fergus. The King buys him off; then Illan makes a sortie and fights with Conchubar's son who has his father's magic shield. When Illan strikes the shield it roars; and Conal Cearnach, far off in his fort, hears the roar and rushes to the defense of his King. Unaware of what the King is doing, Conal slays Illan with a stroke in the back. The dying boy reproaches Conal for helping in the treachery against the sons of Usnach; and Conal in fury because of his own doing thereupon kills the King's son and withdraws in sorrow. One after the other, Ainle and Ardan and Naisi make sorties and

[256] *Ibid.*, p. 60.

kill men by the score. At last, when the Red Branch House is fired, the three brothers with Deirdre in their midst make a last rush to escape. Such is their might and the terror of their flashing swords that they are captured only through the magic of Cathbad, the King's uncle and his Druid, who makes the brothers believe they are swimming in a viscid sea.

The three are brought before the King, who orders their death. But only one man, Maini Rough Hand, will consent to be their executioner; and he will slay the three because Naisi had killed his father and two brothers.

And he said that he himself would kill the sons of Usnach. "If so," says Ardan, "let me be killed first, since I am the youngest of the brothers, in order that I may not see my brothers killing." "Let him not be killed, but me," says Ainle. "Let it not be done so," says Naisi, "for I have a sword which Mananan the son of Lear gave me, and it leaves not remains of stroke or blow, and let us three be struck together with it, and we will be killed at once." [257]

So it was done; and afterwards, Deirdre, running up and down in distraction and grief, met Cuchulin who asked her the name of the slayer. She told him; and "after this, Deirdre lay upon the grave and she began to drink their blood abundantly";[258] then she uttered her lament and died.

This version of O'Flanagan's [259] was so well done that it provided some of the writers of the late nineteenth century revival

---

[257] "Deirdri," p. 107. Cf. James Stephens, *Deirdre*, p. 285; Lady Gregory, *Cuchulain of Muirthemne*, London, 1915, pp. 133-34. Lady Gregory's version is almost word for word from O'Flanagan's.

[258] "Deirdri," p. 115.

[259] Douglas Hyde, *Literary History*, pp. 303-4, *n.* 3, says, "O'Flanagan first printed two versions of it the Deirdre story . . . the older of these two versions agrees closely with that contained in ms. Egerton 1782 . . . but neither of the mss. he used is now known to exist." Dr. Hyde ignores the facts that O'Flanagan supplied the beginning of his first version from Keating, and that all of his second "historical" version (*Trans. Gaelic Soc.*, pp. 145-78) is practically the same as that in O'Connor's Keating (ed. 1723, pp. 175-79).

not only with the outline of the story but also with actual phrasing and imagery. Deirdre's lament on leaving her exile in Alba has, for instance, these lines in O'Flanagan:

> Sweet is the cuckoo's note on bending bough
> On the cliff over the vale of the two Roes.[260]

Lady Gregory has "sweet is the voice of the cuckoo on the bending branch on the hill above Glen-da-Rua"; [261] and Douglas Hyde gives it "sweet the voice of the cuckoo upon bending bough upon the cliff above Glendarua." [262] Again, when Barach puts obligations on Fergus to attend his feast the latter, in O'Flanagan's phrase, becomes "a reddened crimson bulk from head to foot." [263] These words Lady Gregory makes into "reddened with anger from head to foot"; [264] and James Stephens renders "became one purple mass from the crown of his head to the soles of his feet." [265] Examples could easily be multiplied; the influence is clear and unmistakable.

*   *   *   *   *   *   *   *   *   *

With the work of O'Flanagan, this part of our history of Irish poetry comes to a close. One of the main paths of that poetry will trace its beginnings in the work of these early historians and translators. In a few years that path will have as mileposts the work of Jeremiah John Callanan (1795–1829), Edward Walsh (1805–50), James Clarence Mangan (1803–49), and Sir Samuel Ferguson (1810–86). It was the ability of the first-named of these that moved W. B. Yeats to say that "An honest style did not come into English-speaking Ireland until

---

[260] "Deirdri," *Transactions of the Gaelic Society*, p. 51.

[261] *Op. cit.*, p. 121.

[262] *Op. cit.*, p. 312.

[263] *Op. cit.*, p. 53.

[264] *Op. cit.*, p. 121.

[265] *Op. cit.*, p. 200. It might be noted here that Sir Samuel Ferguson in *Deirdre: a One-Act Drama*, acknowledges O'Flanagan's work in his introduction.

Callanan wrote three or four naive translations from the Gaelic." [266] But consideration of these men lies outside our scope.

[266] *A Book of Irish Verse*, London, 1900, introductory essay, p. xix.

Bibliography

PRIMARY SOURCES

Abbott, T. K. and Gwynn, E. J., *Catalogue of the Irish Manuscripts in the Library of Trinity College, Dublin*. Dublin, 1921.

A Catalogue of the Bradshaw Collection of Irish Books in the University Library Cambridge. 3 vols., Cambridge, 1916.

A Catalogue of the Lansdowne Manuscripts in the British Museum. London, 1819.

Anthologia Hibernica. Dublin, 1793–1794.

Archdall, Mervyn, *Monasticon Hibernicum*. Dublin, 1786.

A Sermon Preached at Christ-Church, Dublin, 27th June, 1762 before the incorporated Society for promoting English Protestant Schools in Ireland. Dublin, 1762.

A Sermon Preached before the Society Corresponding with the Incorporated Society in Dublin for promoting English Protestant Working-Schools in Ireland, by Thomas, Lord Bishop of Oxford. London, 1757.

Ayscough, Samuel, *A Catalogue of the Manuscripts . . . in the British Museum*. 2 vols., London, 1782.

Barnes, Wm., ed., *A Glossary; With some pieces of verse of the Old Dialect of the English Colony in . . . Forth and Bargy. Formerly collected by Jacob Poole*. London, 1867.

Book of Howth in *Calendar of the Carew Manuscripts,* Vol. V. London, 1871.

Brooke, Charlotte, *Reliques of Irish Poetry*. Dublin, 1789; 2nd ed., Dublin, 1816.

Calendar of State Papers Relating to Ireland, 1574–1585. London, 1867.

Calendar of the State Papers Relating to Ireland, 1601–1603. With Addenda, 1565–1654, and of the Hanmer Papers. London, 1912.

Chetwood, W. R., ed., *A Tour Through Ireland . . .* by two English Gentlemen. 2nd ed., Dublin, 1748.

Concanen, Matthew, *Miscellaneous Poems . . . by Several Hands*. London, 1724.

Cox, Sir Richard, *Hibernia Anglicana: or, the History of Ireland from the Conquest thereof by the English, To this present Time*.

With an Introductory Discourse touching the Ancient State of that Kingdom. London, 1689.

Critical Review. Vol. LXX, London, 1790.

Daly, John, ed., *The Kings of the Race of Eibhear.* A Chronological Poem, by John O'Dugan, with a translation by Michael Kearney, A. D. 1635. Dublin, 1847.

Davies, Sir John, *A Discovery of the State of Ireland.* London, 1613.

Dermody, Thomas, *The Harp of Erin.* 2 vols., London, 1804.

Derrick, John, *The Image of Ireland with a Discoverie of the Woodkarne.* London, 1581; rptd Edinburgh, 1883, with notes by Sir Walter Scott. Scott had originally published it in his edition of Lord Somer's *Tracts,* London, 1809.

Dix, E. R. M'Clintock, *Catalogue of Early Dublin Printed Books, 1601–1700.* 2 vols., Dublin, 1898.

Dublin Penny Journal. 1832–33.

Dugdale, Sir William, *Monasticon Anglicanum.* 3 vols., London, 1655–1673; rptd London, 1849.

Edkins, Joshua, *A Collection of Poems.* 2 vols., Dublin, 1789–90.

European Magazine and London Review. Vol. II, London, 1782.

Farewell, James, *The Irish Hudibras, or Fingallian Prince, Taken from the Sixth Book of Virgil's Aenaeids, and Adapted to the Present Times.* London, 1689.

Gilbert, Sir John T., *Facsimiles of the National Manuscripts of Ireland,* Pt. IV. Vol. I, London, 1882.

Hardiman, James, *Irish Minstrelsy, or Bardic Remains of Ireland, with English Poetical Translations.* 2 vols., London, 1831.

Harris, Walter, ed., *Hibernica: or some antient pieces relating to Ireland.* 2 parts, Dublin, 1747–50.

Harris, Walter, ed. and trans., *The Whole Works of Sir James Ware Concerning Ireland.* 3 vols., Dublin, 1739–64.

Hely, James, trans., *Ogygia* [written originally in Latin by Roderick O'Flaherty in 1685]. Dublin, 1793.

Historical Manuscripts Commission, Tenth Report, Appendix, Pt. V. Vol. XIV, London, 1885.

Hutchinson, Francis, *A Defence of the Antient Historians . . . of Ireland and Great Britain.* Dublin, 1734.

James, M. R. and Jenkins, Claude, *A Descriptive Catalogue of the Manuscripts in the Library of Lambeth Palace.* Cambridge, 1930.

Keating, Geoffrey, *A General History of Ireland* [written originally in Gaelic about 1640].

 trans. by Dermod O'Connor. London, 1723.

 trans. by William Halliday. Vol. I, Dublin, 1811.

 trans. by John O'Mahoney. New York, 1857.

 trans. by Patrick Weston Joyce. Book I, Part I, Dublin, 1900.

 trans. by David Comyn and Patrick S. Dineen. The Irish Texts Society, London, 1902, 1908, 1914.

MacCurtin, Hugh, *A Brief Discourse in Vindication of the Antiquity of Ireland*. Dublin, 1717.

Moffet, Wm., *Hesperi-neso-graphia: or, the Western Isle Described*. London, 1724.

Monthly Review, series 2, vol. IV. London, 1791.

Moryson, Fynes, *An Itinerary*. London, 1616; rptd Glasgow, 1907, 4 vols.

Mozeen, Thomas, *A Collection of Miscellaneous Essays*. London, 1762.

Murphy, Denis, ed., *The Annals of Clonmacnoise*. Trans. by Conall Mageoghegan in 1627. Dublin, 1896.

Nicholson, Wm., *Irish Historical Library*. London, 1724.

O'Conor, Charles, *Dissertations on the History of Ireland*. Dublin, 1753; 2nd ed., Dublin, 1766.

O'Flanagan, Theophilus, trans., *Cambrensis Refuted: or rather Historical Credit in the Affairs of Ireland Taken from Giraldus Cambrensis by Gratianus Lucius*. Dublin, 1795.

O'Grady, Standish Hayes and Flower, Robin, *Catalogue of Irish Manuscripts in the British Museum*. 2 vols., London, 1926.

O'Grady, Standish James, *History of Ireland*. Dublin, 1878-80.

O'Halloran, Sylvester, *A General History of Ireland*. 2 vols., London, 1788.

O'Reilly, Edward, *A Chronological Account of nearly Four Hundred Irish Writers*. Iberno-Celtic Soc. Trans., Vol. I, pt. 1, Dublin, 1820.

Ritson, Joseph, *A Select Collection of English Songs*. 3 vols., London, 1783.

Ritson, Joseph, *English Anthology*. 3 vols., London, 1793-94.

Scott, Sir Walter, *The Works of Jonathan Swift*. London, 1814; 2nd ed., 19 vols., Boston, 1883.

Shaw, William, *A Gaelic and English Dictionary*. London, 1780.

Spenser, Edmund, *Works.* Ed. Collier, 5 vols., London, 1862.

Stanihurst, Richard, "A Treatise containing an Plaine and Perfect Description of Ireland," in Holinshed's *Chronicles,* London, 1578; rptd London, 1808, Vol. VI.

The Gentleman's Magazine, and Historical Chronicle. Vol. XXI, London, 1752.

Transactions of the Gaelic Society of Dublin. Dublin, 1808.

Transactions of the Ossianic Society. Vol. I, Dublin, 1854.

Transactions of the Royal Irish Academy. Dublin, 1787, *et. seq.*

Vallancey, Charles, *A Grammar of the Iberno-Celtic, or Irish Language.* Dublin, 1773.

Vallancey, Charles, ed., *Collectanea de Rebus Hibernicis.* 6 vols., Dublin, 1770–1804.

Walker, Joseph Cooper, *Historical Memoirs of the Irish Bards.* London, 1786; 2nd ed., 2 vols., Dublin, 1818.

Walsh, Peter, *A Prospect of the State of Ireland.* London, 1682.

Ware, Sir James, ed., *Ancient Irish Histories of Spenser, Campion, Hanmer, and Marleburrough.* 2 vols., Dublin, 1633; rptd Dublin, 1809.

Warner, Fernando, *History of Ireland.* 2 vols., London, 1763.

Watkinson, John, M.D., *A Philosophical Survey of the South of Ireland.* London, 1777.

Whyte, Laurence, *Original Poems on Various Subjects, Serious and Diverting.* Dublin, 1740; 2nd ed., Dublin, 1742.

Whyte, Samuel, ed., *The Shamrock: or, Hibernian Cresses.* Dublin, 1772; 2nd ed., Dublin, 1792–94.

Winne, J. H., *A Compleat History of Ireland.* 2 vols., London, 1774.

Young, Arthur, *Tour in Ireland.* London, 1780.

SECONDARY SOURCES

Anglia. LVII, 1933.

Arber, Edward, ed., *The English Scholar's Library of Old and Modern Works,* # *10.* London, 1880.

Bateson, F. W., ed., *Cambridge Bibliography of English Literature.* Vol. III, New York, 1941.

Best, Richard Irvine, *Bibliography of Irish Philology and of Printed Irish Literature.* Dublin, 1913.

Boyd, Ernest, *Ireland's Literary Renaissance*. New York, 1916.

Colum, Padraic, *The Story of Lowry Maen*. New York, 1937.

Corkery, Daniel, *The Hidden Ireland*. Dublin, 1925.

Croker, T. Crofton, *Fairy Legends and Traditions of the South of Ireland*. 3 parts, London, 1825–28.

Croker, T. Crofton, *Researches in the South of Ireland*. London, 1824.

Croker, T. Crofton, ed., *Popular Songs of Ireland*. London, 1839; Morley's Universal Library Edition, London, 1886.

Croker, T. Crofton, ed., "Historical Songs of Ireland." *Percy Society Publications,* Vol. I, London, 1840; "A Kerry Pastoral." *Percy Society Publications,* Vol. VII, London, 1842; "Popular Songs, illustrative of the French invasions of Ireland." *Percy Society Publications,* Vol. XXI, London, 1845.

Crone, John S., *A Concise Dictionary of Irish Biography*. London, 1928.

Curtis, Edmund, *A History of Medieval Ireland*. London, 1923.

Curtis, Edmund, *A History of Ireland*. London, 1937.

de Blacam, Aodh, *Gaelic Literature Surveyed*. Dublin, 1929.

de Blacam, Aodh, *A First Book of Irish Literature*. Dublin, 1936.

Dictionary of National Biography.

Dix, E. R. M'Clintock, "Humfrey Powell, the First Dublin Printer." *Proceedings of the Royal Irish Academy,* XXVIII (August 1908), C, 7, 213–16.

Duffy, Sir Charles Gavan, *The Ballad Poetry of Ireland*. Dublin, 1843; 3rd ed., Dublin, 1845.

Dunn, Joseph, *The Ancient Irish Epic Tale, Tain Bo Cualgne*. London, 1914.

Dunn, Joseph and Lennox, P. J., *The Glories of Ireland*. Washington, 1914.

Elton, Oliver, trans., *The First Nine Books of Saxo Grammaticus*. Folk-lore Society Publications, Vol. XXXIII, London, 1893.

Ferguson, Sir Samuel, "Curiosities of Irish Literature: The Mere Irish." *Dublin University Magazine,* IX (1837), 546–558.

Ferguson, Sir Samuel, *Deirdre: a One-Act Drama*. Dublin, 1880.

Fitzmaurice, E. B. and Little, A. G., *Materials for the History of the Franciscan Province of Ireland, 1230–1450*. Manchester, 1920.

Fleay, F. G., *A Biographical Chronicle of the English Drama, 1559–1642*. London, 1891.

Gilbert, Sir John T., *A History of the City of Dublin*. 2 vols., Dublin, 1854–59.

Gregory, Lady A., *Cuchulain of Muirthemne: the Story of the Men of the Red Branch of Ulster*. London, 1902.

Gregory, Lady A., *Gods and Fighting Men: the Story of the Tuatha De Danann and of the Fianna of Ireland*. London, 1904.

Gwynn, Stephen, *Irish Literature and Drama*. London, 1936.

Healy, James, *Ireland's Ancient Schools and Scholars*. Dublin, 1897.

Heuser, W., *Die Kildare-Gedichte: die altesten mittelenglischen Denkmäler in anglo-irischer Überlieferung*. Bonner Beitrage zur Anglistik, Heft XIV, Bonn, 1904.

Hinton, Edward M., *Ireland through Tudor Eyes*. Philadelphia, 1935.

Hoare, Dorothy M., *The Works of Morris and Yeats in Relation to Early Saga Literature*. Cambridge, 1937.

Hogan, Jeremiah, *The English Language in Ireland*. London, 1932.

Hull, Eleanor, *A History of Ireland*. 2 vols., London, 1932.

Hyde, Douglas, *A Literary History of Ireland*. New York, 1899.

Jocelin, "A Latin Narrative of the Life and Miracles of St. Patrick." Printed by Thomas Massingham in *Florilegum Insulae Sanctorum*. Paris, 1624.

Jones, Howard Mumford, *The Harp That Once—*. New York, 1937.

Joyce, Patrick Weston, *Old Celtic Romances*. London, 1879; 2nd ed., London, 1894.

Kenny, James F., *The Sources for the Early History of Ireland*. Vol. I, Ecclesiastical, New York, 1929.

Kittredge, G. L., *Early English Poems and Lives of Saints*. Berlin, 1896.

Law, Hugh Alexander, *Anglo-Irish Literature*. Dublin, 1926.

Lecky, W. E. H., *A History of Ireland in the Eighteenth Century*. 5 vols., Boston, 1893.

Lowndes, William Thomas, *The Bibliographer's Manual of English Literature*. London, 1834; Bohn's edition, London, 1857–64.

Lydgate, John, *Fall of Princes*. Edited by Henry Bergen for the Carnegie Institute of Washington, D.C., publication #262, 4 parts, Washington, D.C., 1923–27.

MacCulloch, John A., *The Mythology of all Races,* Vol. III, "Celtic." Boston, 1918.

MacLysaght, Edward, *Irish Life in the Seventeenth Century: After Cromwell*. London, 1939.

McCarthy, Justin, ed., *Irish Literature*. 10 vols., New York, 1904.

McGee, Thomas D'Arcy, *Irish Writers of the Seventeenth Century*. Dublin, 1846.

M'Lauchlan, Thomas, *The Dean of Lismore's Book*. Edinburgh, 1862.

Mezger, Fritz, *Der Ire in der englischen Literatur bis zum Anfang des 19. Jahrhunderts*. Leipzig, 1929.

Montgomery, Henry R., *Specimens of the Early Native Poetry of Ireland*. Dublin, 1846; new edition, Dublin, 1892.

Moore, Thomas, *Memoirs of Richard Brinsley Sheridan*. London, 1827.

Nason, A. H., *James Shirley, Dramatist*. New York, 1915.

Newell, E. J., *A History of the Welsh Church*. London, 1895.

O'Curry, Eugene, *Lectures on the Manuscript Materials of Ancient Irish History*. Dublin, 1861.

O'Curry, Eugene, *On the Manners and Customs of the Ancient Irish*. 3 vols., Dublin, 1861.

O'Donoghue, D. J., *Poets of Ireland*. Dublin, 1912.

O'Grady, Standish Hayes, *Silva Gadelica*. 2 vols., London, 1892.

O'Rahilly, Cecile, *Ireland and Wales, their historical and literary relations*. London, 1924.

Revue Celtique, Vol. XXXII. Paris, 1911.

Ryan, Desmond, *The Sword of Light*. London, 1939.

Ryan, Richard, *Biographia Hibernica*. Dublin, 1819.

Savage, John, *'98 and '48*. New York, 1860.

Seymour, Aaron Crosley, "A Memoir of Her Life and Writings," prefixed to Charlotte Brooke's *Reliques of Irish Poetry,* 2nd ed., Dublin, 1816.

Seymour, St. John, *Anglo-Irish Literature, 1200–1582*. Cambridge, 1929.

Slover, Clark Harris, "Early Literary Channels between Great Britain and Ireland." *University of Texas Studies in English,* No. 6 (December 1926), pp. 5–52; No. 7 (November 1927), pp. 5–11.

Snyder, E. D., *The Celtic Revival in English Literature 1760–1800*. Cambridge, 1923.

Stephens, James, *Irish Fairy Tales*. New York, 1923.

Stephens, James, *Deirdre*. New York, 1923.

Wells, John Edwin, *A Manual of the Writings in Middle English 1050–1400*. New Haven, 1916.

Williams, Harold, *The Poems of Jonathan Swift*. 3 vols., London, 1937.

Wright, Thomas, *Reliquiae Antiquae*. 2 vols., London, 1841–43.

Wright, Thomas, *Saint Patrick's Purgatory*. London, 1844.

Yeats, W. B., *The Wanderings of Oisin and Other Poems*. London, 1889.

Yeats, W. B., *A Book of Irish Verse*. London, 1895; 2nd ed., London, 1900.

Yeats, W. B., *Autobiographies*. New York, 1927.

Yeats, W. B., *Collected Plays*. New York, 1933.

Yeats, W. B., *Collected Poems*. New York, 1933.

Index